Pie
in the Sky

a delicious cookbook
of luscious puddings

by Glyn Williams

The East Anglian Air Ambulance

Published by: The East Anglian Air Ambulance,
Hangar D, Gambling Close, Norwich Airport, Norfolk NR6 6EG
Charity Registration Number: 1083876

Copyright © East Anglian Air Ambulance 2010

ISBN: 978-0-9566740-0-5

Designed by Mark Shreeve of *season* magazine

Printed in Great Britain by Fuller-Davies,
Hadleigh Road Ind. Est., Ipswich, Suffolk IP2 OUF

contents

foreword

The Earl of Iveagh, Trustee of the East Anglian Air Ambulance

It's a great honour to preface the East Anglian Air Ambulance Cookbook, **Pie in the Sky**, dedicating it to our highly skilled aircrew and all the illustrious doctors and paramedics, who have saved the lives of so many.

I have maintained a close connection to the charity for many years and continue to be humbled by the fantastic work that the team carries out. The charity serves these parts with a first class service, often at times of dire personal need.

Thanks to all those people with tremendous culinary talent who have whisked up these great recipes. I am sure most will take a little longer than the Air Ambulance's twelve minutes it has for maximum delivery time of a casualty to the nearest A & E facility!

Every copy of this book sold helps to keep those life-saving rotors spinning. Thank you for contributing to the Air Ambulance's mission and may you enjoy these fantastic recipes, designed to keep the wolf well away from the door.

Edward
Elveden, Norfolk

by **Glyn Williams**
local food editor
and unabashed pudding lover

introduction

Pie in the Sky, n. *A flight of fancy, a grand scheme
or a frivolous confection*

Few things in life make us smile like a great pudding or decadent
dessert... Something comforting like a family favourite for Sunday
lunch, perhaps a steaming treacle sponge or jam roly poly... Or to
impress your dinner party guests, something indulgent and elegant,
maybe a rich chocolate soufflé or a fancy pavlova...

When I was asked by the East Anglian Air Ambulance, a great cause
close to my heart, to help with this pudding-themed cookbook, to be
called **Pie in the Sky**, it did seem, well, somewhat 'pie in the sky'.

But now, six months on, after a speedy team effort, bags of united
enthusiasm and lots of help from some well known celebrities, the great
East Anglian public and many of the region's best chefs - it is no longer,
well only in name, **Pie in the Sky**.

What a delicious creation, full of sweet things mixed together with love,
finished to near perfection by talented craftspeople, it is definitely a
yummy tribute to the wonderful food we enjoy here in the Eastern
counties.

Everyone has their weakness for a good pud, even those who claim not
to have a sweet tooth. A decadent dessert always puts a smile on faces,
including the most satiated diner. However, I must say, more often than
not, Christmas pudding does usually prove an indulgence too far – but I
do recommend it for Boxing Day breakfast! Take your slices of plum
pud, dust well with icing sugar and pan fry in butter, perfect alongside
a full English as a festive hangover cure.

As I was sitting contemplating about writing these few words of introduction, I caught the end of a BBC Radio 4 discussion and they were talking all things 'afters', including two definite savoury-toothed celebrities who wouldn't admit to eating dessert. But eventually both succumbed to reluctantly declaring their favourites, a proper old fashioned rice pudding for one and a perfect crème brûlée for the other. Oh, how even the staunchest weaken all too easily when it comes to a good pud...

All too often whilst writing this book, I have been asked for own favourite desserts, so here goes... Bakewell tart and fresh raspberries or plum crumble and proper custard would both be high on my list, but in first place it would be vanilla pannacotta with red wine poached pear.

Let's hope 'Pie in the Sky' flies off the shelves for this wonderful cause. And as they say, 'the proof of the pudding is in the eating' so head to it.

Happy reading and glorious feasting

God bless, Glyn

PS I must mention Simi McGeorge's wonderful brownie recipe (below right) entered into our competition to find the best public pudding recipes. I am not sure if it was given tongue-in-cheek but it certainly amused us so we wanted to share it with you!

Measurements

1 tbsp = 1 tablespoon
1 dsp = 1 dessertspoon
1 tsp = 1 teaspoon
(spoonfuls are all level unless stated)

ml = millilitres
g = grams
kg = kilograms

Oven temperatures given are for non-fan ovens unless stated otherwise. Individual ovens vary greatly in hotness – adjust temperatures according to the particular tendency of your own.

Cooking times are approximate – remove dishes earlier or cook them for longer, depending on whether the desired results have been achieved in colour and texture or if the dish has cooked sufficiently.

Pay attention to the dangers of sharp knives and other kitchen equipment eg food processors, mixers and blenders, using extra caution to avoid injury.

Take care when dealing with hot ingredients or dishes, especially if attending to items heating on the hob or being removed / put into the oven.

All recipes have been professionally tested and given in good faith – responsibility cannot be taken for consequences of typological errors during the publication process.

Accompanying images are pictorial illustrations and not necessarily exact representations of the final recipe instructions.

Simi's Altitude Brownies

This is my recipe for chocolate brownies which I learnt while living in the French Alps. At 1800 metres, things cook differently, so a soft boiled egg takes 7 minutes instead of 3. This recipe is absolutely amazing, a chocolate brownie never tasted so good and, with the addition of walnuts, makes it a very grown up dessert. I have tried this recipe at normal altitude but it does not work at all and I'm yet to come across a recipe that produces brownies as good as these!!

250g of 75% or over dark chocolate
250g of brown sugar
125g of yogurt
125g plain flour
80g melted butter
2 eggs
2 handfuls of walnuts, roughly chopped

Pre-heat the oven to 180c. Melt the chocolate in a bain-marie with 30g of the butter. Melt the remaining butter and leave to one side. Add the yogurt, flour, sugar and eggs to the chocolate and mix together thoroughly, then add the melted butter and the walnuts and give it a final mix. Pour into a deep greaseproof paper-lined tin. Bake until just cooked and leave to rest for 10 minutes. I always serve them warm with strawberries and a luxury vanilla ice cream. Yum, yum, yum! Try it next time you're up a mountain...

East Anglian Air Ambulance

The EAAA operates a 365 day-a-year life-saving service across Bedfordshire, Cambridgeshire, Norfolk and Suffolk. It receives no government or National Lottery funding and has to raise some £4 million each year – that's roughly £10,000 every day – to keep its two air ambulances flying and to provide the advanced medical equipment they carry. We are entirely dependent on your fund-raising and donations, the generous people of the Eastern counties.

Started in 2000, the EAAA was founded to attend accidents and emergencies because the nature of the region's roads often make it difficult for land ambulances to reach the scene of accidents and emergencies quickly. East Anglia has a population of 2.4 million people and covers a vast area, some 5,000 square miles, over a tenth of England, containing some of its most rural and isolated terrain. The EAAA works with the East of England Ambulance NHS Trust to ensure the quickest, most effective and safest method of patient transport is used.

The charity originally operated in Norfolk, Cambridgeshire and Suffolk functioning with just one helicopter - Anglia One. In 2007 we extended our service to operate a second helicopter - Anglia Two, which serves Bedfordshire and Cambridgeshire. Anglia One now focusses on serving Norfolk and Suffolk.

The charity is constantly developing its expertise and now uses paramedics with advanced skills, as well as deploying doctors, which enables critical care treatment to be given at the scene to stabilise patients, saving more lives and often sparing more serious long term complications. If necessary, the air ambulances then transports the most serious cases to the most suitable hospital, rather than by road.

The journey aboard the EAAA to the closest A & E Department takes no more than 12 minutes from anywhere in the region; alternatively the helicopter will often divert to a more appropriate specialist centre of medical excellence, eg Addenbrookes Hospital in Cambridge for patients needing neurosurgery.

What are the benefits to the patients? When treating victims of trauma or other medical emergencies, the chance of full recovery is greatly increased if they receive definitive medical care within the first hour. The availability of the air ambulance helps ensure that more accident victims are reached and attended to within this critical period.

By buying this book, you are helping to keep our helicopters flying. We value every donation and our patients do even more.
Every mission to a critical injury makes a difference to people's lives. Please keep supporting us – you never know when you or your loved ones might need us.

"The journey aboard the EAAA to the closest A & E Department takes no more than 12 minutes from anywhere in the region."

The Hairy Bikers

Ruth Watson

Tom Parker Bowles

Galton Blackiston

Jean-Christophe Novelli

Amanda Holden

the celebrities

The Hairy Bikers
Strawberry Shrikhand

Better known as The Hairy Bikers, Si (Simon King) and Dave (David Myers) are the hirsute beleathered motorcycling foodies who tour the UK and foreign parts in the pursuit of great food. Despite not being professional chefs, but rather besotted food lovers during their previous behind-the-scenes TV careers, their many credits in front of the camera now include The Hairy Bikers' Cookbook, Twelve Days of Christmas, Mums Know Best, Food Tour of Britain and The Hairy Bakers series.

SERVES 4

250g strawberries
1 dsp balsamic vinegar
1 dsp caster sugar
4 large cardamom pods
250g Greek or thick set yoghurt
Pinch of saffron, soaked in 1 tbsp boiling water
3 tbsp caster sugar
25g flaked almonds, toasted

Firstly, take the tops off the strawberries and halve. Place in a bowl with 1 dsp of caster sugar and the balsamic. Cover with clingfilm and leave to steep for several hours or even overnight.

Remove the seeds from the cardamom pods and crush the seeds in a pestle and mortar.

In a bowl mix together the yoghurt, cardamom seed, saffron (with soaking water) and remaining caster sugar. Mix the whole lot together.

Divide the strawberries into four sundae glasses. Top with the shrikhand and sprinkle with the toasted almonds. Serve with something crisp and biscuity on the side.

Ruth Watson

'Sod it' hot bitter chocolate mousse

SERVES 6

200g bitter chocolate (70% cocoa), roughly broken
100g unsalted butter
6 large eggs, separated
100g caster sugar
30g cocoa powder

to serve, thick Jersey cream

Preheat a fan oven to 180c.

Melt the chocolate and butter together in a bowl over a saucepan of simmering water, in a bain-marie or in the microwave oven.

Whisk or beat the egg yolks and sugar together for a good 5 minutes or until the mixture has doubled in volume and is soft and voluptuous. Fold in the cocoa powder. Add the melted chocolate and butter mixture and whisk for just long enough to combine.

In a very clean bowl, whisk the egg whites until they form just soft peaks (not ultra shiny and stiff as you would for meringues).

Add a quarter of the egg whites to the chocolate mixture and whisk to combine. Using a large kitchen spoon, gently fold in the remaining egg whites, keeping as much air in the mixture as possible.

Lightly butter six 10cm soufflé dishes or similar and spoon in the chocolate mixture, leaving 1cm at the top of the dishes. Put onto a heavy baking sheet and cook the mousses for about 10 minutes until they have risen.

Remove and dust the tops lightly with a little sifted cocoa powder. Serve immediately, spooning the cream into the middle.

Chef, hotelier and now broadcaster by profession, Ruth Watson's trademark no-nonsense approach strikes a resonant chord on her programmes, C4's Country House Rescue and Ruth Watson's Hotel Rescue (and Five's The Hotel Inspector). Co-owner of The Crown and Castle in Orford – W: www.crownandcastle.co.uk – a delightful hotel on East Suffolk's atmospheric coast, Ruth is also an award-winning food correspondent and has written three best-selling books. By her own admission, Ruth is also greedy and likes eating, a lot, and yes, that's deliberately ambiguous...

Tom Parker Bowles

Gooseberry Fool

A regular presenter on Good Food Channel's Market Kitchen, Tom Parker Bowles is an impassioned supporter of ethical sustainable farming, native food and real seasonal ingredients. Well known for his food columns in The Mail on Sunday and Tatler, Tom's books include Full English: A Journey through the British and their Food, The Year of Eating Dangerously: A Global Adventure in Search of Culinary Adventures, and E is for Eating: An Alphabet of Greed. Tom's parents are Camilla, Duchess of Cornwall and Andrew Parker Bowles.

SERVES 4

450g gooseberries
150ml elderflower cordial
150ml milk
1 vanilla pod, split
2 egg yolks
1 tsp arrowroot
30g sugar
150ml double cream, whipped

to serve, brandy snaps or shortbread

Top and tail the gooseberries and put them in a saucepan with the elderflower cordial.

Bring to the boil and then simmer gently for about 30 minutes until soft and pulpy. Leave to cool before transferring to a large bowl.

Heat the milk in a saucepan with the vanilla pod until very hot but not boiling.

Beat the egg yolks, arrowroot and sugar together in a heatproof bowl. Pour in the hot milk, whisk well and return the mixture to the pan on the heat. Remove the vanilla pod and stir the custard gently whilst heating until it thickens, taking care not to let it boil. Pour into a cold bowl and leave to cool.

When the custard is completely cool, pour it over the gooseberries and stir in the whipped cream.

Divide between individual bowls or glasses and serve with home-made brandy snaps or shortbread.

Galton Blackiston
Coffee Meringue with Summer Fruits

SERVES 8

75g icing sugar
2 heaped tsp instant coffee powder
4 egg whites
110g caster sugar
425ml double cream
450g summer fruits, such as strawberries,
  raspberries, blueberries and redcurrants

Pre-heat the oven to 140c.

Sift together the icing sugar and coffee powder
and set aside.

In a spotlessly clean bowl (best in a food mixer),
whisk the egg whites until they have increased in
volume and started to stiffen. Whisking, slowly add
the caster sugar and continue until stiff-peak stage.

With a slotted metal spoon, vigorously beat in the
sifted icing sugar and coffee powder until the
mixture is glossy.

Spoon the meringue on to the centre of a large baking
tray lined with good-quality greaseproof paper.
Spread it out into a circle 25-30cm in diameter and
2-3cm thick.

Place the meringue in the centre of the oven and
bake for about 1½ hours, by which time it should
look cracked on top but still be slightly soft in the
centre. Remove from the oven and allow to cool.

Carefully lift the meringue off the greaseproof
paper and place on a large serving plate. Whip the
cream until it just holds its shape, then spread loosely
over the meringue.

Scatter the summer fruits liberally on top and serve.

Hailing from North
Norfolk, Galton Blackiston
is one of East Anglia's
most familiar TV chefs.
An ardent fan of all things
about his native county, it
is not just wonderful local
ingredients he loves such
as the freshest seafood,
game and samphire but
also Norwich City Football
Club; his dedication to the
Canaries running deep.
Owner with his wife Tracy
of the Michelin starred
Morston Hall –
www.morstonhall.com –
he has become a well
known face on cookery
shows such as Good
Food Channel's Market
Kitchen, BBC2's Great
British Menu and ITV1's
Ten Mile Menu.

Jean-Christophe Novelli

Baked apple soufflés with chocolate and kirsch sauce

SERVES 4

120g raspberry jam
35ml kirsch
15g cornflour
4 very large baking
  apples
100g butter, softened
100g bitter chocolate
  (70% cocoa), grated

8 medium egg whites
300g white chocolate,
  broken into pieces
400ml double cream
100g caster sugar
Icing sugar

Preheat the oven to 180c.

Gently heat the jam until melted and add half the kirsch. In a small bowl, stir the cornflour into a little cold water until dissolved. Add to the hot jam mixture and stir well until thickened, remove from the heat and allow to cool in a large bowl.

Cut off the apple tops and then hollow out the centres, keeping the sides intact but discarding the insides. Drain the apples upside down for 10 minutes and place in a greased ovenproof dish. Butter the insides of the apple shells very carefully and then sprinkle with the bitter chocolate.

Whisk the egg whites stiffly and carefully fold into the jam. Spoon this into the apple cavities and run a knife around the rim of the apple so that the soufflé will rise when baked. Bake in the preheated oven for 8-10 minutes or until the filling has risen fully.

Meanwhile, melt the white chocolate in a bowl over, but not touching, a pan of simmering water. Once melted, stir in the remaining kirsch and cream. Pour into a serving jug.

Serve the apple soufflés hot and dusted with icing sugar, offering the sauce on the side.

Dubbed "the nation's favourite French chef" and past holder of a Michelin star and Five AA Rosettes, Jean – Christophe Novelli now runs one of the country's most respected cookery schools. Once head chef for the late great Keith Floyd, JCN spent nearly a decade building a group of leading restaurants in London. He is an accomplished television presenter, having broadcast on many prime-time celebrity shows across the globe and has written two fabulous books, Everyday Novelli and Novelli: Your Place or Mine?

Amanda Holden

Banana daiquiri Eton mess with strawberry prosecco

SERVES 6

Eton Mess
200ml double cream
200ml crème fraiche
6 meringue nests
5 not-too-ripe bananas
3 tbsp fresh lime juice
2 tbsp white rum
2 tbsp banana liqueur
2 tsp vanilla extract

Strawberries
100g strawberries,
  chopped
Grated zest and juice
  of a large lime
4 tbsp icing sugar
3 tbsp prosecco

You can make the strawberry mix and daiquiri cream ahead but the remainder of the recipe must be done just before serving.

Place the strawberries in a sieve for a few minutes to remove excess juice. Put into a large bowl and fold in the icing sugar, lime zest and juice. Chill ready for use.

Whip the cream and crème fraiche until it forms soft peaks and beat in the vanilla and a tablespoon each of lime juice, white rum and liqueur. Refrigerate until needed.

Purée three of the bananas with a tablespoon of rum and liqueur. Cut the other two bananas into thin diagonal slices. Gently coat well with two tablespoons of lime juice. Roughly break up meringues by hand.

In a very large bowl, carefully fold together the meringues, banana purée, banana slices and the cream mixture until it looks just mixed and swirled.

Serve into pretty dishes. Mix the prosecco into the strawberries quickly and spoon over the Eton mess. Serve with plenty more rum or fizzy!

Needing little or no introduction, Amanda Holden is perhaps best known as a much adored TV presenter but has also frequently starred as a versatile character actress in the cinema and on the small screen. A household name, she is a very familiar face to the British public, not least as a judge on ITV1's hit show Britain's Got Talent as well as taking centre-stage hosting prestigious award ceremonies. An adopted local, Amanda loves North Norfolk and lives near Burnham Market.

24

the public

Steamed raspberry sponge by Ann Dunning of Gorleston

Grease a large pudding basin and place raspberries into the bottom. Fill an electric kettle with water and boil.

Using an electric food mixer, cream butter and sugar until light and creamy. Stir the vanilla into the beaten eggs. Add a third of the flour and beaten egg to the butter-sugar mixture, beat well and repeat twice until all has been added. Slowly add in enough milk to achieve a thick dropping consistency. Pour over raspberries in the basin.

Put a sheet of greaseproof paper on top of a piece of kitchen foil. Butter well and pleat in the centre. Cover the basin with this and secure well with a doubled length of string (adding a secure string handle helps with removal once cooked).

Put into a suitably deep saucepan, adding enough boiling water to come two-thirds up the sides. Cover and bring to a simmer. Cook for 2 – 2½ hours, checking the water level frequently, until firm and risen.

Serve with pouring cream, crème fraiche or ice cream as well as fresh raspberry sauce or conserve.

SERVES 4

700g fresh raspberries,
   washed and drained.
75g butter
75g caster sugar
2 large eggs, beaten
¼ tsp vanilla extract

150g self raising flour
Full cream milk

Chocolate mousse cake

by Rachael Rudge of Ipswich

Pre-heat oven to 200c. In a food processor, blend together the almonds, marzipan, biscuits, eggs and zest.

Line an 8 inch/22cm loose bottomed tin with baking parchment and spread the marzipan mixture over the base. Bake for about 25 minutes until golden and then cool.

Melt the chocolate in a bowl over hot water. Stiffly whisk the egg whites. Whip together the cream and sugar to a soft peak stage and stir in the chocolate. Fold the chocolate cream into the egg whites. Spread over the biscuit base and chill for 3 - 4 hours, removing from the tin once cold.

Serve with a quenelle of crème fraiche, raspberry coulis and fresh berries.

SERVES 6 - 8

Base
100g ground almonds
200g white marzipan,
   chilled and grated
50g ratafia biscuits,
   crushed
2 eggs
Zest of 1 orange,
   finely chopped

Mousse
225g chocolate
300ml double cream
25g caster sugar
2 egg whites

Surprise sponge pudding

by June Gaught of Thetford

SERVES 4 - 6

Base
25g soft butter
25g soft brown sugar
Juice and flesh of 1 lemon

Sponge topping
110g soft butter
110g caster sugar
2 large free range eggs, beaten
110g self raising flour, sifted
Zest of 1 lemon
Full cream milk

To serve, plenty of cream, perhaps
clotted or chantilly

Take an oblong ovenproof dish and grease well.
Preheat oven to 180c.

Dot the butter over the dish, sprinkle in the lemon
juice and flesh as well as the brown sugar.

Fill an electric kettle and put on to boil.

Using an electric food mixer to make the sponge
topping, beat together the butter and sugar until
light and creamy. Next beat in the eggs a little at a
time. Add in the flour and zest, folding in well.
Finally drizzle in sufficient milk until it becomes a
thick dropping consistency.

Put spoonfuls of the topping over the base of the dish
gently and level out. Slowly and very carefully pour
over a half pint of boiling water. Cook for 30 minutes
or until cooked – the top will look browned and
bounce back when gently pushed.

Serve with your choice of fresh cream, perhaps
clotted or chantilly (whipped up with icing sugar).

"It may seem strange to pour boiling water over the sponge mix but it works – a lovely sauce will be at the base of the pudding when it is cooked" writes June.
"It also works well with just cooked tender rhubarb pieces laid under the sponge topping before baking."

Hot chocolate sponge pudding with mocha sauce

by Kathy Taylor of Bedford

Pre-heat oven to 160c fan or equivalent.

Cream together the butter and sugar in a large bowl. Mix in the cocoa, eggs and flour until the mixture is a thick consistency. Mix in a splash of milk. Place sponge mixture into a greased ovenproof dish, approx 25 x 17cm.

Carefully whisk sauce ingredients together and pour slowly over the sponge mixture.

Bake for 30 – 40 minutes until the top is cooked and sauce is bubbling around the edges.

Serve with good quality vanilla or chocolate ice cream, thick cream or very healthy zero fat Greek yoghurt.

SERVES 8

Sponge
225g butter
225g caster sugar
40g cocoa
4 medium eggs,
   lightly beaten
225g self raising flour
Splash of milk

Sauce
25g good quality
   instant coffee
25g cocoa
110g caster sugar
275ml boiling water

Norfolk syllabub

by Zena Skinner of Bedford

SERVES 6

275ml double cream
75g caster sugar
3 tbsp lemon juice
3 tbsp whisky
Zest of 2 lemons, finely
   chopped

25g hazelnuts, finely
   chopped
25g plain chocolate,
   finely grated
Grated chocolate and/or
   glacé lemon peel for
   garnish

In a basin, softly whip the cream and sugar together. Add the lemon juice and whisky very slowly, whilst whipping with a fork, being careful not to overbeat. Fold in the lemon zest, hazelnuts and chocolate.

Split between 6 chilled glasses and refrigerate for 4 - 6 hours before finishing.

To serve, garnish with more grated chocolate and/or glacé lemon peel.

Frangipani cake

by Alison Cook of Witnesham

"On our recent travels to Australia we discovered the beautiful frangipani shrub" says Alison. "Grown in hot climates all over the world, this is our interpretation of the fragrance of this flower in a cake form. It makes a rich treat for afternoon tea. With suitable accompaniments such as almond ice cream or lemon sorbet, it would make an elegant dessert."

SERVES 4 - 6

Pastry
275g plain flour
150g icing sugar
175g unsalted butter
2 free range eggs, lightly beaten

Filling
150g butter
150g margarine
4 large free range eggs
100g plain flour
300g ground almonds
250g homemade or good quality lemon curd

Topping
300g icing sugar
2 tsp warm water
1 vanilla pod

To make the pastry: place the flour and icing sugar in a bowl or food processor and rub or pulse in butter until the mixture resembles breadcrumbs. Add eggs and mix well. Turn out and knead lightly to make a firm dough. Clingfilm and chill the dough for 30 minutes. Pre-heat oven to 180c.

For the filling: beat butter and sugar until light and creamy, gradually beat in the eggs, then fold in the flour and almonds.

To make the cake, grease and line a 9 inch springform tin with greaseproof paper.

Roll out pastry to fit the tin and gently ease into the base and around the sides. Spread lemon curd over the base and spoon on the filling. Trim pastry to suit. Bake for 50 - 60 minutes or until firm to the touch. Cool in the tin.

Finish with the topping by mixing icing sugar and warm water together with the seeds from the vanilla pod. Spread over the cooled cake. Once set, remove the cake from the tin and serve in hearty wedges.

Spiced orange pudding by Sarah Paul of Cambridge

The day before, place the first four ingredients in a small pan. Scrub oranges in warm water and dry. Remove the zest and reserve the fruit. Finely chop the zest and stir into pan. Cook gently for 3 minutes. Remove from the heat, cover and leave overnight to infuse the flavours.

On the day, pre-heat the oven to 180c. Lightly grease 4 ramekins with unsalted butter and cut the bread into 12 rounds of the same diameter. Squeeze the juice of 2 oranges, adding it to the syrup mixture and warm again for 3 minutes. Cut the skin off the other 2 oranges. Next slice alongside the skin on each side of the segments to remove them without pith.

Build 3 layers of segments and syrup-drizzled bread in each ramekin. Beat the eggs and milk together, then pour over to just cover the bread layers and leave to soak for 30 minutes. Sprinkle over the sugar and dot with butter. Place the ramekins in a deep roasting tray with enough boiling water to reach halfway up the dishes. Bake for 45 - 50 minutes until puffed and golden.

Serve with your choice of cream or ice cream.

SERVES 4

125ml golden syrup
$1/2$ tsp ground coriander
$1/2$ tsp ground cardamom
1 tsp Angostura bitters
4 medium oranges
Unsalted butter
12 slices of white bread, crusts removed
2 medium eggs
400ml semi-skimmed milk
25g demerara sugar

to serve, Cointreau chantilly or good vanilla ice cream

Walnut slice by Lumilla Graham of Hadleigh

Pre-heat oven to 170c.

For the pastry – rub the flour and butter together or pulse in a food processor until fine crumbs. Fold in the sugar and add the egg yolk. Bring together to a pastry dough. Wrap in clingfilm and chill for 30 minutes.

Line a swiss roll tin with non-stick baking parchment. Roll out the pastry (to fit) and place into the tin. Spread the pastry gently with redcurrant jelly. Whisk together the egg yolks and sugar until light and fluffy. Add water and mix again. Fold in the ground walnuts. Whisk the egg whites until soft peaks and fold in.

Spread mixture over pastry. Bake for approximately 30 minutes until cooked and lightly browned. Leave to cool and slice into squares.

SERVES 6

Pastry
200g plain flour
125g unsalted butter, chilled
1 tbsp caster sugar
1 egg yolk

Filling
Redcurrant jelly
4 egg yolks
150g caster sugar
1 tbsp cold water
150g ground walnuts
5 egg whites

Madeira surprise

by Ken Jackson of Sheringham

SERVES 6

Cake
150g butter
150g caster sugar
3 large eggs
125g self raising flour
100g plain flour
Pinch of salt
Grated zest and juice of half a lemon
Glacé lemon peel (optional)

Egg Custard
575ml of milk
25g of butter
a strip of lemon zest
2 whole egg
2 egg yolks

Best quality raspberry conserve
40g sultanas
2 egg whites
100g caster sugar

Pre-heat an oven to 170c. Grease a 7 inch cake tin and line with greaseproof paper. Beat the butter and sugar together until light and fluffy. Beat in the eggs well, one at a time. Fold in the sieved flour and salt alternately with a little of the lemon zest and juice. Put the mixture into the tin, level and decorate with glacé peel. Bake for 1 – 1¼ hours. Cool for ten minutes and then carefully turn out onto a wire rack.

Scald the milk and lemon zest in a saucepan until steaming well, but not boiling. Remove from heat. Whisk together the eggs and yolks in a heatproof bowl, add a few tablespoons of the hot milk and whisk immediately. Pour into a clean saucepan and heat whilst stirring until a coating consistency.

Pre-heat the oven to 180c.

Slice the cake into thick slices, spread generously with conserve and line the base and sides of a medium ovenproof dish. Sprinkle with sultanas and pour over the custard gently. Stand the dish in a deep wide roasting tray. Pour boiling water around until a third of the way up the dish sides. Bake for 35 minutes until golden brown and allow to cool.

For the meringue, whisk the egg whites until they are soft peaks, add sugar one spoonful at a time, whisking between each, until stiffly peaked. Pipe the pudding top with the meringue. Using a blowtorch or a very hot grill, carefully brown all over.

Ken's poem for the cookbook recipe competition –
"My madeira surprise is a sight for sore eyes, a delight for the palate as well, a neat little sweet, a veritable treat, all those who eat it do tell the best I have eaten, it cannot be beaten, and my dearest wish, with a word to the wise, is that East Anglia's best dish is my madeira surprise"

39

Chocolate fondant

by Maureen Pinner of Easton

SERVES 6

175g plain chocolate, broken up
175g unsalted butter
4 whole large eggs
4 egg yolks
75g caster sugar
75g plain flour

to serve, real vanilla ice cream

Pre-heat the oven to 190ºC.

Place the chocolate and butter in a heatproof bowl and melt together over a saucepan of simmering water. Remove and allow to cool to room temperature, stirring occasionally.

Whisk eggs, yolks and sugar together until they have doubled in volume (best done in an electric mixer). Gradually fold in the chocolate mixture until thoroughly mixed.

Add in the sifted flour and gently fold together well.

Spoon the mixture into 6 greased ramekins. Bake in the oven for 8 – 9 minutes (the outside should feel just firm to the gentle touch).

Best served in the ramekins and topped with a scoop of your best, preferably home made, vanilla ice cream.

Editor's note: This recipe contains undercooked egg mixture so is best avoided by the vulnerable, eg the sick, pregnant and young children. Alternatively increase the cooking time until they are fully cooked through and leaves a skewer clean – but this will be chocolate sponge, which misses some of the magic saucery.

"You can refrigerate this recipe before cooking in the ramekins on the day, or store in a container for up to one week. It makes a very convenient dinner party pudding with a lovely gooey molten centre" says Maureen. "Serving them in the ramekins is easier but if you are feeling arty, they can be cooked in dariole moulds and turned out carefully onto serving plates."

Apple almond pie

by Joan Valsler of Ipswich

Pre-heat the oven to 180c. Place the rice and milk in a saucepan with 25g of the sugar and stir whilst bringing to a gentle boil. Simmer gently for about 15 minutes or until the rice is tender. Spoon over the base of a large pie dish.

For the pastry, rub the butter into the sieved flour until rough breadcrumb texture. Stir in 50g each of the almonds and sugar, then bind with the egg to a soft dough. Leave in the fridge for 45 minutes.

Spread the apples over the rice. Mix together the remaining 25g of both sugar and almonds and sprinkle over the apples, followed by the cider.

Roll out the pastry carefully and cover the pie dish. Brush with milk and scatter with sugar.

Bake for 25 minutes, then cover with foil, and return to the oven for another 30 – 35 minutes until it looks cooked and golden.

Serve warm with pouring cream or vanilla custard.

SERVES 4 - 6

50g pudding rice
400ml milk
100g butter
175g plain flour
75g ground almonds
100g caster sugar
1 egg, beaten
700g cooking apples, peeled
  and sliced
4 tbsp cider
Milk and sugar to glaze

Chocolate hazelnut roulade

by Sarah Clark of Bottisham

Pre-heat a fan oven to 120c. Line a swiss roll tin with baking parchment paper. Whisk egg whites until stiff. Add half the caster sugar and repeat. Add remaining sugar and repeat.

Whisk in the cornflour and vinegar. Spread the meringue into the tin and level the top. Bake for 45 minutes and remove from oven, leaving it to cool in the tin.

Whip up the double cream until thick. Spread half the hazelnuts on greaseproof paper. Turn meringue out onto nuts and peel off the parchment. Spread meringue with praline spread and whipped cream. Sprinkle over remaining nuts.

Roll up the meringue gently using the greaseproof to control it and transfer onto a serving dish. Dust with icing sugar.

Serve with lots of chocolate sauce and vanilla ice cream.

SERVES 6

4 egg whites
225g caster sugar
1 tsp cornflour
1 tsp white wine
  vinegar
110g finely chopped
  hazelnuts
Praline spread to taste
275ml double cream

to serve, icing sugar
  for dusting, vanilla
  ice cream and dark
  chocolate sauce

43

Marmalade and whisky brioche bread and butter pudding
by Sue Jones of Tasburgh

SERVES 8

110g raisins
110ml whisky
3 large eggs
1 egg yolk
1 tsp vanilla extract
100g caster sugar
400ml full cream milk
300ml double cream
Pinch of sea salt
250g brioche, thickly
  sliced and halved
40g butter
8 tbsp good quality dark
  marmalade

to serve, marmalade
  and clotted cream

The day before, put the raisins in a small saucepan and add the whisky. Bring to a simmer, then immediately turn off the heat and leave to soak overnight.

The day after, pre-heat the oven to 180c. Beat the whole eggs, egg yolk, vanilla and sugar together in a large heatproof bowl. In a heavy bottomed pan, bring the milk, cream and a pinch of salt gently to a simmer whilst stirring. Take off the heat and whisk into the egg mixture.

Butter the brioche and spread with marmalade. Place a single layer of brioche, marmalade side up, in an ovenproof dish and sprinkle on some of the raisins and juices, then repeat. You should end up with two or three layers, depending on the size of the dish. Pour on the custard through a sieve and leave for half an hour to allow it to soak.

Before baking, make sure that there are no bits of fruit sticking out of the custard as they will burn. Cook for 25-30 minutes until golden brown.

Do not serve burning hot, allow to relax for 15 minutes. It eats well with a glaze of melted marmalade alongwith a good dollop of clotted cream.

45

the local chefs

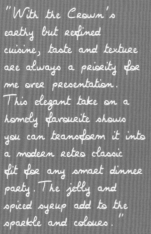

"With the Crown's earthy but refined cuisine, taste and texture are always a priority for me over presentation. This elegant take on a homely favourite shows you can transform it into a modern retro classic fit for any smart dinner party. The jelly and spiced syrup add to the sparkle and colours."

Stephen David, The Crown at Woodbridge
Baked strawberry mascarpone cheesecake with Pimm's jelly and minted red chilli syrup

SERVES 6+

250g ginger biscuits
80g unsalted butter
300g hulled strawberries
4 eggs
175g caster sugar
Grated zest of 1 lime
1 tbsp honey
2 tsp vanilla extract
500g mascarpone
200g crème fraîche

Pimm's Jelly
125g caster sugar
350ml cold water
1 sprig fresh mint
75ml Pimm's
75ml fresh lemon juice
5 leaves gelatine

Minted Red Chilli Syrup
250ml water
250g caster sugar
1 red chilli, roughly chopped
2 sprigs fresh mint, shredded

to serve, mascarpone

Grease an 18cm springform tin. Crush the biscuits, melt the butter and mix well together. Pour into the prepared tin and press down. Refrigerate until set.

Finely dice 150g of strawberries and drain. Pre-heat fan oven to 170c. Whisk together eggs, sugar, zest, honey, vanilla, mascarpone and crème fraîche until smooth. Gently fold in the strawberries. Spoon mix onto the biscuit base and cook in the oven for 45 minutes until light golden. Cover with a tea towel to cool for an hour or more and refrigerate in the tin.

Run a hot palette knife around the sides and remove tin. Slice remaining strawberries and cover the top.

In a saucepan dissolve the sugar with the water and mint by stirring over a hot heat. Remove to one side. Soften the gelatine in cold water for 5 minutes. Once drained, whisk into the sugar solution until dissolved. Mix in the lemon juice and Pimm's. Strain and pour into an oiled baking tray to set.

For the syrup, stir together all the ingredients over a gentle simmer for 5 minutes. Strain and chill.

To serve, cut the cheesecake into wedges (using a warm knife) and serve with a quenelle of mascarpone, cubes of Pimm's jelly and a drizzle of minted chilli syrup.

A boutique townhouse inn, The Crown at Woodbridge is a cosmopolitan combination of chic dining rooms, buzzy glass-roofed bar (complete with suspended boat) and ten calming designer bedrooms. 21st century cutting-edge interiors, indulgent luxury and modern comforts combine with 16th century architecture. Previously Executive Chef of The Hoste Arms, North Norfolk's famous celebrity haunt, Chef-Patron Stephen David owned Earsham Street Café in Bungay, Suffolk before arriving in Woodbridge with his trademark style of gutsy flavourful yet elegant cooking. Adnams and Greenwich Meantime ales, great eclectic wines, funky hidden sun terrace, informal eating on squidgy sofas and low tables, all complete the picture. The Crown at Woodbridge was named National winner of 2010 Alastair Sawday's 'Pub with Rooms' award.
The Crown at Woodbridge, Thoroughfare, Woodbridge, Suffolk IP12 1AD
T: 01394 384242 W: www.thecrownatwoodbridge.co.uk

Chris Lee at The Bildeston Crown
Lemon Tart

SERVES 8+

Pastry case
100g sugar
100g butter
2 eggs, beaten
250g plain flour

Lemon filling
Zest of 4 lemons
Juice of 9 lemons
500g sugar
17 eggs
1 egg yolk
1 litre double cream
2 tbsp unsalted butter

Pre-heat the oven to 170c. Cream the butter and the sugar well, then slowly add in the eggs. Add the flour, mixing it as little as possible until just incorporated. Remove, wrap in clingfilm and refrigerate for an hour. Roll out thinly and line a large high-sided springform cake tin, ensuring there are no holes. Chill for another 30 minutes. Blind bake the case for 35 minutes. Remove the tin from the oven to cool.

Reduce oven temperature to 100c. In a large saucepan, bring the zest, juice and sugar to the boil whilst stirring. Remove from heat and put to one side.

Beat together the cream, eggs and yolk. Pour the contents into the saucepan whilst whisking. Allow to cool and pass through a sieve. Pull out oven bars a little and sit the tart on them. Pour in the mixture until close to the top. Push the bars back in gently and cook for around 45 minutes or until the mix is cooked but not completely set.

Remove from the oven and run a knife carefully between the edges of the lemon mix and pastry to stop it from cracking. Once cooled and before serving, dust the top with icing sugar and lightly brown it carefully with a blowtorch or under a very hot grill.

Sitting proudly in the centre of genteel Bildeston with a backdrop of rural Suffolk, The Bildeston Crown is a former coaching inn, restored by local farmer and businessman James Buckle in 2003. With the help of Chris and Hayley Lee, Head Chef and General Manager, it has been transformed into a luxury hotel and destination restaurant. But it has still kept much of its historical charm with its period feel and an atmospheric bar whilst upstairs twelve indulgent en-suite bedrooms would satisfy the most sophisticated travellers. Very much the centre of attention, Chris Lee prides himself on using the best quality produce for his exciting cooking, much of it sourced from the Buckles' farm such as excellent Suffolk Red Poll beef. The Bildeston Crown is well renowned - Gold Award winner 'Taste of England', AA Three Red Stars and Three Rosettes, Good Food Guide UK Up-and-Coming Chef 2008 award, Best Small East of England Hotel 2008. The Times restaurant reviewer, Giles Coren, called The Bildeston Crown "the best little progressive kitchen in Suffolk" and in February 2009, Chris beat Si and Dave on The Hairy Bikers' Tour of Britain! **The Bildeston Crown, High Street, Bildeston, Suffolk IP7 7EB**
T: 01449 740510 W: www.thebildestoncrown.com

"This dish, with its various elements, is one of my favourites. At The Bildeston Crown, I like to serve it with lemon curd, lime posset and orange sorbet. Much of my food is in this "assiette" style as I like working with the different tastes and textures in several ways to tease the palate. Here we are all about surprises and variations on citrus flavours.

nb If you can make the other garnishes, that's great but if not, choose your favourite tart fruit accompaniments."

"Our reworked variation of a River Café classic. The raspberries add a surprising extra depth of flavour and subtlety, which does justice to the original but takes it to an alternative dimension"

Simon Cadge at The Old Bridge Hotel
'Chocolate Nemesis'

SERVES 6+

250g fresh raspberries
750g caster sugar
650g dark 70% cocoa
  chocolate, chunked
450g butter
10 large eggs

to serve, crème fraiche and
  dark chocolate sauce

Very gently stir and simmer the raspberries in 150ml of cold water and 50g of sugar for a few minutes. Boil the mixture whilst stirring to reduce it down to half its volume.

Over a large heavy bowl, press the pan contents through a sieve until a coulis drops through, discarding the seeds.

Pre-heat the oven to 160c, line a 27cm approx springform cake tin with foil and put a full kettle on to boil.

Melt chocolate and butter together in a bowl over, but not touching, simmering water. Remove from the heat and allow to cool. Beat together the eggs and remaining sugar with an electric mixer for five minutes until they have quadrupled in volume. Fold the chocolate and butter mixture thoroughly into the egg - sugar mixture. Then, very gently, add the raspberry coulis, stirring just once or twice.

Pour the mixture into the prepared cake tin and sit the tin in a large deep roasting tray. Transfer to the oven shelf and then pour enough boiling water around the tray to come three-quarters up the tin sides. Bake for one hour, then turn the oven off and allow to cool completely before removing.

Serve in wedges with a quenelle of crème fraiche on the side and drizzled with chocolate sauce.

A handsome, ivy-clad 18th century property on the banks of the River Ouse, yet right on the edge of the town centre, The Old Bridge has that rare elusive atmosphere of a professionally run townhouse hotel and a relaxed, bustling inn. Its air of escapism makes it a popular destination for fine dining and indulgent stays as well as a bolthole for the local community. John Hoskins MW as the hotel's dedicated owner shares his passions with an erudite appreciation of great wine – indeed he was the first Master of Wine on the British restaurant scene. His description of The Old Bridge's appeal is apt: "whether you use us for a great cappuccino, a pint of Adnams, a chilled glass of Billecart-Salmon Champagne, a BLT, a gourmet dinner, scones with Jersey cream, a not-too-boring business meeting, or even a wild night away – I hope you enjoy yourselves."
The Old Bridge Hotel, Restaurant and Wine Shop, 1 High Street, Huntingdon, Cambs PE29 3TQ T: 01480 458410 W: www.huntsbridge.com

Eden Derrick at The Wildebeest Arms
Warm Banana Bread with Earl Grey Poached Prunes and Vanilla Ice Cream

SERVES 6

Poached Prunes
300g caster sugar
300ml water
1 cinnamon stick
1 vanilla pod, split
2 earl grey teabags
200g stoned dried prunes

Banana Bread
450g muscovado sugar
450g butter
4 very ripe medium size bananas
175g sultanas
125g toasted walnut halves
6 large eggs
175g self raising flour, sifted
175g plain flour

to serve, very good vanilla ice cream

The day before, start the poached prunes. Take a saucepan and add the sugar, water, cinnamon, vanilla and teabags. Stir well whilst bringing gently to a simmer.

Add the prunes, stir and bring back to a good simmer. Remove from the heat, allow to cool, cover and refrigerate. Allow to come to room temperature before using the next day.

For the cake, pre-heat oven to 200c. Cream together the muscovado sugar and butter until light and fluffy.

Roughly chop the walnuts. Mash the bananas. Fold banana and walnuts into the sugar-butter mix along with the sultanas. Beat the eggs and add, mixing well. Fold in the flour gently.

Grease a loaf tin and fill with the cake mixture. Bake for 30 – 40 minutes until browned and cooked – test with a skewer.

To serve, slice generously, garnish with whole prunes along with quenelles of ice cream.

Part of Norwich and periphery-based Animal Inns, The Wildebeest Arms was the first and original destination pub-restaurant in Henry Watt's excellent local group. Alongside the city's Mad Moose Arms/1UP restaurant (Warwick Street off Unthank Road), and Mackintosh's Canteen (on Norwich's Chapelfield Plain), recently joined by The Hunny Bell (in Hunworth near Holt), it might stand proud but its bedfellows are snapping at its heels. The popularity of all Henry's establishments is part down to doing things right and perhaps striving harder than their peers; but 15 years have also served The Wildebeest Arms well in establishing it on the Norwich dining scene. And the appreciative audience of South Norfolk's finest who flock here know what they are looking for, a comforting but inspiring mix of mostly familiar favourites: perhaps seared scallops, Jerusalem artichoke velouté, crispy bacon and pea shoots; parmesan crusted smoked haddock, buttery mash, leeks, poached egg, caper-herb nage; dark chocolate fondant, burnt honey ice cream, cognac prunes and chocolate sauce.
The Wildebeest Arms, 82-86 Norwich Road, Stoke Holy Cross, Norwich, NR14 8QJ
T: 01508 492497 W: www.thewildebeest.co.uk

"This versatile banana bread recipe is garnished as an elegant dessert but it is also lovely for afternoon tea. And if you want to be more elaborate, it can be dipped in spiced egg custard and then fried in butter for 'pain perdu'. Why not try it as a base of a very decadent bread and butter pudding... Nb You can add other favourite dried fruit such as apricots or dates instead of the sultanas. The poached prunes make a good garnish as a smooth purée. And you don't have to stick to vanilla ice cream, why not try home-made rum and raisin or stem ginger ?"

"A traditional family favourite of mine, I chose rice pudding because for me it evokes all those wonderful memories of childhood and a classic comfort dish. But as with much of our food, we love to give things a twist, so by adding the spiced tuile biscuit and the fruitiness of the peaches, it becomes more of a restaurant dessert rather than a homely pud - it's delicious! Nb This dish can be made ahead, refrigerated and warmed to serve or even eaten at room temperature."

Stuart Oliver at milsoms Kesgrave Hall
Baked rice pudding with roasted peaches and spiced tuile biscuits

SERVES 4

Rice Pudding

100g pudding rice
600ml full fat milk
115g sugar
1/2 vanilla pod, split and
   scraped
zest of 1/2 lemon
100ml double cream
150g tin evaporated milk
freshly grated nutmeg,
   to taste

Tuile Biscuit

50g butter, softened
50g icing sugar
50g egg whites
50g plain flour, sieved
Szechuan peppercorns,
   toasted and ground

Roasted Peaches

2 peaches
2 tbsp icing sugar
2 tbsp unsalted butter

First make the rice pudding. Pre-heat the oven to 160c. Place the rice, full fat milk, sugar, vanilla pod and lemon zest into an ovenproof pan and bring to a gentle simmer whilst stirring. Cover rice with a circle of parchment paper and put into the oven to bake for 20 minutes or until the rice is soft. Remove from the oven and stir in the cream and evaporated milk. Find the vanilla pod and remove. Sprinkle with nutmeg.

For the biscuits, pre-heat the oven to 170c. In a large bowl, cream together the butter and icing sugar until light and fluffy. Whisk in the egg whites gradually and then fold in the sifted flour. Using a palette knife, spread thinly into 7cm circles on a lightly greased non-stick baking sheet. Sprinkle with Szechuan pepper. Bake for 5 minutes until golden brown. Whilst still hot, after a few seconds, remove carefully with the palette knife and lay over a rolling pin to set and cool. Store in an airtight container.

Lastly, prepare the peaches. Pre-heat the oven to 200c. Halve the peaches and remove the stones. Place in an ovenproof gratin dish and put a good knob of butter in each half. Dust well with icing sugar. Bake for 20 minutes until soft.

To serve, divide the rice pudding into shallow soup plates, place a peach half on each side and top with a tuile.

A Georgian mansion set in 38 acres of parkland and woods, milsoms Kesgrave Hall is the Ipswich outpost of the Dedham original with modern relaxed brasserie dining, inside and out, and luxurious 'wow factor' bedrooms. With excellent party and meeting rooms, it stylishly and sumptuously offers all the facilities and enjoyment of a traditional hotel without the stuffiness – all day opening offering the whole menu and a 'no rush, no need to book' formula. An AA 3 Star hotel and with one AA Rosette for its restaurant, milsoms was named 'Suffolk Hotel of the Year' in 2009. Head Chef Stuart Oliver champions local produce and guests can watch the theatre of his dedicated team at work through the open plan kitchen. Eating alfresco in such beautiful surroundings is a delight, even in the rain, under the huge architectural sail on the heated terrace.
milsoms Kesgrave Hall, Hall Road, Kesgrave, Ipswich, Suffolk IP5 2PU
T: 01473 333741 W: www.milsomhotels.com/kesgravehall

James Preston at The Broad House Hotel
Iced orange parfait with poached rhubarb and ginger crumble

SERVES 6+

Orange Parfait
4 large eggs, separated
Juice and zest of 2 medium oranges
200g caster sugar
175ml double cream

Crumble
150g plain flour
100g salted butter, diced
100g demerara sugar
20g rolled oats
1 tsp ground ginger

Rhubarb
8 rhubarb sticks, cut into thin fingers
250g caster sugar
500ml water

The day before, make the parfait. Place the egg yolks and 100g of the caster sugar in a large heatproof bowl over simmering water. Whisk the mixture until light, fluffy and tripled in volume. Once stiffened, remove the bowl and set aside to cool.

Weigh 80g of egg whites, place in a very large bowl and add the remaining caster sugar. Whisk into a stiff peak meringue. In a third bowl, whip the cream with the finely chopped orange zest to soft peaks. Fold the orange cream gradually into the meringue. Then fold this into the yolk mixture. Pour into an oiled, clingfilm-lined loaf tin. Cover and freeze overnight.

For the crumble, pre-heat the oven to 170c. Rub the flour and butter together until breadcrumb stage. Stir in the sugar, oats and ginger. Bake on a baking tray for around 20 minutes until golden brown. Remove and once cooled, break into a crumble.

For the rhubarb, simmer sugar and water whilst stirring. Place rhubarb in a heatproof bowl and pour over hot sugar syrup. Cover and leave for 20 minutes. Remove fruit from syrup and leave to cool.

To serve, remove clingfilm from parfait and slice generously. Roll each portion in crumble to coat. Top with rhubarb sticks, orange and mint if available.

The Broad House Hotel was opened in autumn 2007 having been converted from an idyllic country estate with tranquil parkland and river frontage on the Broads. Elegant weddings in fairytale surroundings and nine indulgent suites and bedrooms give added appeal. Creative flair is a theme of the fine dining on offer, making the best use of local Norfolk ingredients and the excellent salads, vegetables and fruits produced by the hotel's green-fingered gardeners. Having trained in the county, James Preston has been very loyal to Norfolk throughout his career, arriving at The Broad House in 2009 before being shortly promoted to Head Chef. A typical meal might be slow cooked curried duck with a carrot and orange salad, natural yoghurt and onion bhaji; wild sea trout with brown crab puffs and a samphire, courgette and potato salad; Broad House 'arctic roll', strawberries, jelly and mint.
Broad House Hotel, The Avenue, Wroxham, Norfolk NR12 8TS
T: 01603 783567 W: www.broadhousehotel.co.uk

"We are lucky to have rhubarb flourishing in our walled garden at the Broad House so this was an obvious choice for me. The parfait is a lovely cooling end to a summer supper alfresco and orange, rhubarb and ginger work well together as flavours."

"Dinner party dishes should sound interesting, look attractive and taste delicious but, of course, also be quick to prepare. This basil pannacotta is all of that, as well as versatile, because you can change it very easily with different flavours; mint or lemon thyme instead of basil, for example. Nb My favourite garnishes for the pannacotta are crumbled pistachio meringue and a strawberry champagne jelly, which are relatively easy for the home chef to produce."

Jason Waterfield at King's College
Basil cream pannacotta – pictured with strawberry champagne jelly and pistachio meringue crumble

SERVES 4

2 1/2 gelatine leaves
180ml cold milk
200ml double cream
50g caster sugar
2 small handfuls of
  basil leaves

Soak the gelatine leaves in the cold milk for five minutes before draining in a sieve, also reserving the milk. Stir the cream and sugar together in a pan and bring gently to the boil.

Add the basil leaves (retain a couple of the smaller leaves to garnish) and bring back to a simmer. Take off the heat and when just warm, pour into a blender. Add the soft gelatine and blitz until smooth. Strain the cream mixture into a large jug and whisk in the milk.

Fill 4 ramekins with the mixture and refrigerate for 6 – 8 hours to set.

Before serving, place the ramekins into a deep roasting tray and carefully pour hot water around (not over) the dishes until nearly to the top. After a few seconds, pour off water carefully and invert the ramekins on to dessert plates and lift off, releasing the pannacotta.

Serve with your choice of garnishes, chosen for colour and texture.

Few buildings in the East of England can compete with the grandeur of King's College, one of the world-famous educational establishments making up the University of Cambridge. Its impressive setting lends itself to society catering with innovative food and immaculate service with such a beautiful backdrop; the Queen was entertained here in prestigious style to mark the University's recent 800th anniversary. When Jason Waterfield joined King's some seven years ago as Director of Catering and Executive Chef, his vision was to replicate the college's reputation for academic excellence within the catering department.
Before coming to Cambridge, Jason worked in London's five star hotels and more unique venues with his first head chef position, aged just 24, at Mayfair's Westbury Hotel.
His dedicated King's team frequently provide banqueting for high-profile occasions, cooking at a fine restaurant quality for up to 300 guests in the college's magnificent vaulted hall.
King's College, King's Parade, Cambridge Cambs CB2 1ST
T: 01223 331410 W: www.kings.cam.ac.uk/venue

David Grimwood at The Froize, Chillesford

Suffolk summer berries set in a rosé wine jelly with clotted cream ice cream and strawberry sauce

SERVES 4

450g halved strawberries
375ml good rosé wine
  (we use Spanish Navarra)
65g caster sugar
3 gelatine leaves

200g hulled strawberries
30-50g caster sugar, to taste
1-2 tsp lemon juice, to taste

5 large free range egg yolks
110g caster sugar
300ml clotted cream
150ml whole milk

First make the jelly. Heat the wine and sugar together whilst stirring until fully dissolved. Soak gelatine for 5 minutes in cold water to soften. Strain the gelatine and whisk it into the wine syrup. Leave to cool. Place the strawberries into suitable moulds or ramekins and pour over the jelly mixture. Refrigerate until set and required.

For the strawberry sauce - place the strawberries in a food processor and whiz to a liquid. Blend in sufficient sugar and lemon juice until glossy and dissolved, to suit your liking. Refrigerate until needed.

To make the ice cream, whisk the egg yolks and sugar in a food mixer until light and creamy. Scald well the cream and milk in a saucepan whilst stirring over a medium heat. Gently pour the cream mixture into the food mixer whilst whisking. Reheat the mixture gently in a clean saucepan whilst stirring with a wooden spoon until it thickens to a coating texture. Sieve and leave to cool. Churn in an ice cream machine until ready and freeze until required.

To serve, turn the jellies out of their moulds and garnish with quenelles of ice cream and strawberry sauce.

Chef/Proprietor David Grimwood enthuses "The Froize is all about good food, good company and the best of local ingredients. I have been cooking at the stoves of Suffolk for over 35 years and I believe that this experience shows in the food we serve and in the number of friends who have dined with me over those decades in three different pubs. Chillesford is a bit in the sticks, a lovely drive out on a sunny lunchtime and even in the worst weather, my lovely loyal regulars come hell or high water. I think that I am the most loyal supporter of the wonderful ingredients we produce in Suffolk, especially around me on the coast here. We are blessed with some of the best farmers and add to that fresh fish, superb game, bartered fruit and excellent vegetables, it makes my life so much more enjoyable as a chef."
The Froize Inn, Main Road, Chillesford,Woodbridge, Suffolk IP12 3PU
T:01394 450282 W: www.froize.co.uk

"This little fun dessert epitomises great Suffolk produce for me. Our good friends, the Pool family bring us their perfect fresh berries and other luscious fruit from High House Farm in Sudbourne, the next village a couple of miles down the road. We often have them jellied a few hours after they have been picked, how fresh and local is that..."

"As the name suggests, I developed this recipe in honour of The Duchess of Bedford as the Inn is part of the Woburn Abbey estate. I love nursery puddings, often on our menus – there is nothing like the comforting warming appeal of a steaming dessert. This one is more elegant than your usual syrup sponge and custard, the orange liqueur cream giving that extra finesse."

Olivier Bertho at The Inn at Woburn
Duchess pudding with an orange cream

SERVES 6+

1 carton orange juice
250ml double cream
50ml orange liqueur
350g butter
350g caster sugar
6 eggs, beaten
420g self raising flour
75g raisins
75g chopped glacé cherries
75g candied peel
75g chopped almonds
6 tbsp milk
Few drops almond essence

First start with the orange cream. Bring the juice to the boil in a heavy saucepan and reduce by three-quarters. Add the cream and bring back to the boil. Remove from the heat, stir in the liqueur and cool before refrigerating until needed.

For the pudding - in a food mixer, cream butter and sugar together until light and fluffy. Add in the eggs in a gentle stream, beating well. Sieve the flour and fold gently into the mixture. Next fold in the fruit, peel and almonds. Lastly add enough milk to get a soft dropping consistency. Place the mixture into buttered ramekins and cook in a steamer for $1\frac{1}{2}$ hours or until cooked.

Serve the hot puddings turned out onto plates with the cold orange cream (or warmed if preferred).

Woburn Abbey is one of the great treasure houses in England and has always been at the forefront of income diversification to make best use of the wonderful grounds and properties which form the estate, such as their well-known golf club and safari park. An 18th century hotel, The Inn at Woburn (and Olivier's Restaurant) has been cleverly extended and now offers destination dining and sophisticated accommodation, including very special cottage suites. Excellent banqueting rooms make the hotel a popular wedding venue too.
Olivier Bertho's cuisine is a blend of classic British and French with a twist, novel flair tempered with reassuring familiarity, worthy of its Two AA Rosettes – perhaps starting with basil-crusted carpaccio of Woburn venison with baby rocket and parmesan; main course of monkfish tail with crab ravioli and a white bean and tomato cassoulet; ending with apple and cinnamon cheesecake with rhubarb syrup.
The Inn at Woburn, George Street, Woburn, Beds MK17 9PX
T: 01525 290441 W: www.woburn.co.uk/inn

Richard Hughes at The Lavender House Bitter Chocolate and Sea Salt Caramel Tart

SERVES 6

Pastry
120g icing sugar
200g plain flour
50g cocoa powder
150g butter
1 egg, beaten

Filling
200g soft butter
200g light muscovado sugar
200g double cream
1 tsp Maldon sea salt
150g Venezuelan 70% cocoa
   chocolate, grated

Pre-heat the oven to 180c. Place the icing sugar, plain flour and cocoa into a bowl and rub in the butter. Add in the egg before mixing into a smooth, quite sticky dough.

Wrap the dough into a ball, wrap it in clingfilm and then refrigerate for at least 30 minutes.

Roll out the chilled pastry to 3mm thick and line a springform 20cm tart tin. Chill the pastry case again for 15 minutes and then bake blind for 15 minutes until crisp. Remove and cool.

For the filling, heat the butter and sugar without stirring in a saucepan and when melted, simmer for two minutes.

Add the cream and salt, bring to the boil and simmer for a further five minutes.

Remove from the heat and whisk in the chocolate until this has completely melted.

Carefully pour the mixture into the pastry case and refrigerate until set.

Serve in wedges with your favourite garnishes.

Accomplished author, cookery teacher, entrepreneurial businessman and not forgetting, a very experienced chef and restaurateur, Richard Hughes is a familiar face on the Norfolk food scene. The Lavender House is rightly well known and has received glowing accolades over the years from restaurant guides and press alike. As one of the county's main culinary faces, Richard is often seen in county magazines and newspapers. Indeed, such has been his influence he has been nominated for the 2010 'Outstanding Achievement Award' in the EDP Norfolk Food Awards. Together with Iain Wilson of the famous Byfords in nearby Holt, he co-owns the quirky Pigs pub in Edgefield and they also run the iconic Assembly House venue in Norwich. One of Rick Stein's Food Heroes, Richard often gives cookery demonstrations around the county, runs a cookery school at the restaurant and finds time to regularly produce a new cookery book.
The Lavender House, 39 The Street, Brundall, Norfolk NR13 5AA
T: 01603 712215 W: www.thelavenderhouse.co.uk

"This delicious tart is made with excellent quality chocolate which gives it a rich, deep taste while the sea salt offsets the sweetness of the filling and the pastry. It's a great-looking, adult dessert which can be made as a large tart to share or put into individual cases and decorated on plates for that special occasion. At The Lavender House we serve it with dark chocolate ganache sauce, simple berries and white chocolate curls. Choose whatever you prefer; it also works well with tropical and citrus fruit, fresh or in a compote."

"I chose this sunny colourful dessert because it is quick and simple to make, very summery with its seasonal ingredients and once prepared has lots of style and flavour as well as being light to eat.

Justin Kett at The Brudenell Hotel
White chocolate and raspberry mousse with lemon biscotti

SERVES 6

Mousse
225g white chocolate
  in chunks
40g water
40g caster sugar
40g liquid glucose
2 leaves of gelatine
250ml whipped cream
Approx 30 raspberries

Lemon biscotti
30g melted butter
Zest of 2 lemons
  (reserve juice)
4 whole eggs
310g caster sugar
Good pinch of baking
  powder
450g flour, sifted
300g chopped almonds
  or pistachio nuts
Juice of 2 lemons

First make the mousse. Clingfilm 6 individual ring moulds. Soak the gelatine in cold water. Melt the white chocolate in a large bowl over simmering water. In a heavy saucepan, bring the water, sugar and glucose to the boil whilst stirring. Remove from the heat. Whisk the gelatine into the sugar mixture and then pour this over the white chocolate. Leave to cool slightly whilst whipping the cream until stiff. Fold the chocolate mixture gently but thoroughly into the whipped cream. Place five raspberries into the base of each mould and divide the mousse between them evenly. Refrigerate to set.

Pre-heat fan oven to 150c. For the biscotti, melt the butter and stir in the zest to infuse. Whisk the eggs and sugar until light and creamy, then fold in the baking powder and flour. Now add the nuts, butter (with zest) and juice, folding together thoroughly. Split the mixture into 3 pieces and shape into large cigars. Part bake on lined baking sheets for 30 - 40 minutes. Once the biscotti have cooled, slice wafer thin with a sharp knife, lay out on lined baking sheets and return to the oven until light golden and crisp. Remove the mousse from the moulds and the clingfilm.

To serve, place onto 6 serving plates with the biscotti on the side.

An icon for modern coastal-chic hotels, The Brudenell sits at the southern end of the seafront in quintessentially English Aldeburgh; its top class facilities and indulgence evident in VisitBritain's Four Star Gold Hotel Award. The open plan cocktail bar, relaxing restaurant and alfresco terrace look out over the rolling beach and lapping waves. Head Chef Justin Kett's seafood-led food and seasonal menus play a huge part in The Brudenell's magnetic appeal as a dining destination - meat lovers and vegetarians do well. Moving to East Suffolk several years ago, Justin was previously at the Michelin-starred Castle Hotel in Taunton, Somerset. His elegant well planned cooking sings the freshness of sustainable local produce – perhaps ravioli of Pinney's smoked eel with wilted spinach and champagne sauce; rump of spring lamb with spiced couscous and pak choi; banoffee pie Brudenell style.
The Brudenell Hotel, The Parade, Aldeburgh, Suffolk IP15 5BU
T: 01728 452071 W: www.brudenellhotel.co.uk

Martin Lee of The Plough at Bolnhurst
Rhubarb with Cambridge Burnt Cream

SERVES 6

1kg young rhubarb
Caster sugar
5 free range egg yolks
550ml organic double cream
1 vanilla pod, split

The day before, cut the rhubarb into 1cm pieces and put into a thick bottomed pan with two tablespoons of water.

Bring to a gentle simmer, stirring regularly, and cook until tender. Add sugar to taste, aiming for a more tart than sweet flavour.

Transferring into a sieve or muslin, let the rhubarb drain for three or four hours and then refrigerate.

Put a couple of tablespoons of the resultant thick compote into the bottoms of 6 very shallow dishes.

Scrape the vanilla pod and add the seeds and pod into a heavy saucepan with the cream and bring to the boil.

In a wide jug, whisk together the yolks and 50g of sugar. Add a third of the hot vanilla cream and stir together. Pour this back into the remaining cream and over a low heat, continuously stir with a wooden spoon until a light custard forms and coats the back of the spoon. Sieve into another wide jug and pour carefully over a spoon to almost fill the fruit dishes.

Refrigerate overnight to set the custard. Before serving, sprinkle a thin layer of sugar over the custard and glaze carefully with a blowtorch.

The Tudor roots of The Plough at Bolnhurst are evident in its original features, wonderful beams, few windows and atmospheric low ceilings. Through the open plan kitchen, diners avidly watch Martin and his team of chefs hard at work, working with the wonderful ingredients on their doorstep and more worldly tastes to produce their unique award-winning cuisine. Highly rated as one of the East of England's leading restaurants in major publications such as The Good Food Guide, Harden's and the like, there is nothing wacky about the food, the cleverness is all about the restraint to produce proper, seasonal, interesting, well prepared dishes, evident in artisan home-made bread; crab ravioli with coriander shellfish bisque; braised pork belly with home-made black pudding mash; roast pumpkin tart or red fruit soup with prosecco sorbet. An interesting wine list, convivial ambience and relaxed yet professional service, warmly led by Martin's wife, Jayne and their co-owner Michael Moscrop, make for a rightly popular destination restaurant.
The Plough, Kimbolton Road, Bolnhurst, Beds MK44 2EX
T: 01234 376274 W: www.bolnhurst.com

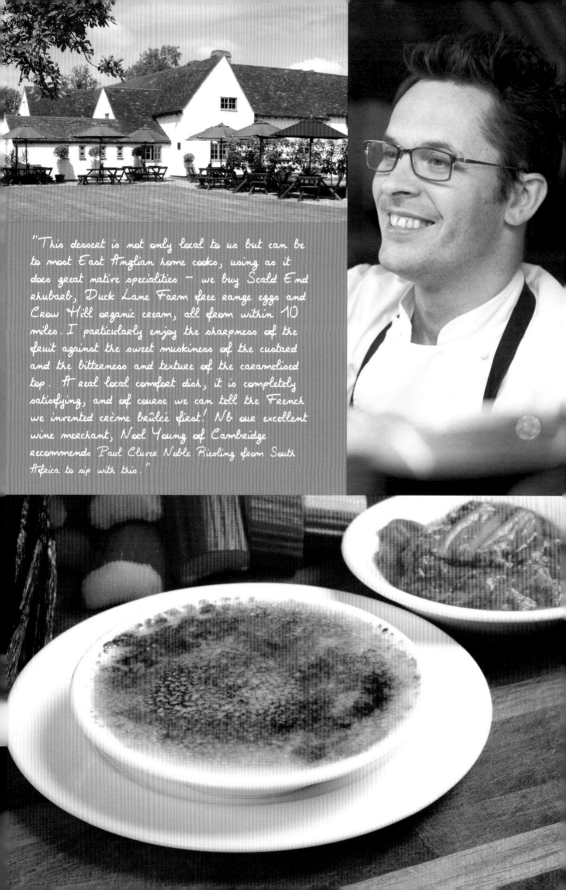

"This dessert is not only local to us but can be to most East Anglian home cooks, using as it does great native specialities — we buy Scald End rhubarb, Duck Lane Farm free range eggs and Crow Hill organic cream, all from within 10 miles. I particularly enjoy the sharpness of the fruit against the sweet muskiness of the custard and the bitterness and texture of the caramelised top. A real local comfort dish, it is completely satisfying, and of course we can tell the French we invented crème brûlée first! Nb our excellent wine merchant, Noel Young of Cambridge recommends Paul Cluver Noble Riesling from South Africa to sip with this."

"The subtle taste of lavender in this light and refreshing dessert is different, helping to cut the richness. We always love to use as many local, seasonal Norfolk ingredients as possible. The smooth pannacotta eats well with something crumbly such as a tuile, if you are feeling arty or just good home-made shortbread."

Harry Kodagoda of The White Horse at Brancaster Staithe
Lavender and local honey pannacotta with a berry and mint compote

SERVES 6+

Pannacotta
1.2 litres double cream
Zest of 1 lemon, chopped
1 vanilla pod
3 tbsp clear runny honey
20g lavender
200 ml milk
6 sheets leaf gelatine
30g icing sugar, sifted

Berry Compote
100g diced strawberries
100g raspberries
50g blueberries
50g redcurrants
100g icing sugar, sifted
40g fresh mint leaves, finely sliced

to serve, your choice of tuile or shortbread biscuits

Start the pannacotta the day before.

Soften the gelatine leaves in cold water for 5 minutes, then strain to remove the water. In a heavy saucepan, stir together the double cream, lemon zest, vanilla pod (split and scraped), honey, lavender and milk and simmer for 5 minutes – do not let it boil. Add the icing sugar and drained gelatine to the pan and stir gently until dissolved.

Sieve the mixture into a large jug and then fill individual dariole moulds. Leave to cool and refrigerate overnight to set.

Make the berry compote one hour before serving. Combine the fruit gently but thoroughly with the sieved icing sugar. Leave to marinade for 1 hour so that the juices start to run, forming a syrup.

When required, dip the dariole moulds into hot water to loosen. Place the pannacottas onto dessert plates and spoon the fruit compote around the sides.

Serve with your choice of tuile or shortbread biscuits.

Few places can claim to have a more magical view on the East Anglian coast than The White Horse at Brancaster Staithe. Diners share the view of the North Norfolk sun setting over the sea as the tide floods in around marsh and dune with seals and circling wildfowl. Discerning visitors and the travel press love the place in equal measure. James Nye and his father Cliff have been impassioned over this wild atmospheric part of the county for decades, evident everywhere you look, taking it from simple local pub to stylish, indulgent destination inn, with well planned hotel accommodation and alfresco terraces front and rear alongside locals' bar and capacious dining areas. The food is one of the key attractions, naturally tapping into all that wonderful Norfolk produce of sea and land – Brancaster oysters served naturally with lemon or in a light beer batter with tartare sauce; confit pork belly and seared scallop with pea purée, apple and black pudding jus; bouillabaisse with saffron potatoes and rouille.
The White Horse, Main Road, Brancaster Staithe, Norfolk PE31 8BY
T: 01485 210262 W: www.whitehorsebrancaster.co.uk

Nick Wilson of The Swan at Lavenham
Apple and Cobnut Cheesecake
with Aspall Cyder Granita

SERVES 6+

Cheesecake base
250g bran flakes
50g praline paste (not spread)
available from Suffolk-based
www.infusions4chefs.co.uk

Cheesecake filling
5 medium egg yolks
700g cream cheese
280g caster sugar
10 gelatine leaves
875ml double cream
400g apple purée
200g cobnuts or hazelnuts,
  lightly toasted

Apple granita
200ml Aspall cyder
100ml water
55g caster sugar

For the cheesecake base, mix the two ingredients to form a stiff but pliable mixture. Roll in between two sheets of baking parchment paper until 5mm thick. Refrigerate until firm for about 1 hour.

For the filling, whisk together the eggs, cream cheese and sugar until smooth and light. Stir in the apple.

Soak the gelatine in cold water for 5 minutes. Heat 25ml of cream in a pan until hot and whisk in the drained gelatine. Once dissolved, sieve to remove any lumps. Whisk into the apple and cheese mixture. Whip the cream until it forms soft peaks and fold in.

Fill the 6 clingfilmed individual ring moulds carefully with the cheesecake mix and smooth off tops. Refrigerate for 6 hours or until needed.

Pulse the nuts in a food processor until they form the consistency of rough crumbs and reserve.

For the granita, heat all the ingredients gently whilst stirring, until the sugar has dissolved. Pour into a suitable plastic container and freeze for approximately 4 hours.

To serve, top the cheesecakes with the crushed nuts and place onto chilled plates, garnished with quenelles of the granita.

A quintessential 'town and country' retreat, the iconic, half-timbered Swan Hotel has stood in medieval Lavenham for over 600 years. Its ancient oak beams and inglenook fireplaces make dining by candlelight decadent in the vaulted timbered restaurant, complete with minstrels' gallery. Befitting its high AA Four Star rating, its charms include 45 cosseting bedrooms including luxurious suites and four posters, the historic Old Bar and alfresco eating on warmer days in tranquil gardens. Head Chef Nick Wilson's experiences working with Jean-Christophe Novelli have stamped their mark with modern British and French influenced cuisine – sautéed spring lamb cutlets with sweetbread soufflé and summer cabbage; Six Churches partridge roasted with liquorice root on confit duck hash; pan roasted East Anglian sea bass, Cromer crab risotto and caramelised butternut squash.
The Swan Hotel, High Street, Lavenham, Suffolk CO10 9QA
T: 01787 247477 W: www.theswanatlavenham.co.uk

"I am always keen to source fine seasonal and local produce so this dish ticks all those boxes in the autumn when our great Suffolk orchards give us such superb apples. Of course, they pair up so well with lovely Aspall cyder. Cobnuts, also called filberts, are a particular type of native hazelnut, but you can replace them with the latter out of season or if your greengrocer cannot get them for you."

"We love pairing food with wines and especially beers, so this recipe combines all our favourites. It has a balance of bitterness, sweetness, creaminess and a variety of textures as well as all those tastes we love, chocolate, nuts and of course great Meantime London stout."

Kevin Honeywell at The Anchor
Stout Mascarpone Mousse and Praline

SERVES 6

Mousse
600ml stout
100g sugar
1 gelatine leaf
200g mascarpone
250ml double cream
2 egg whites

Praline
200g sugar
100g almonds

to serve, chocolate biscuits

For the praline, melt the sugar without stirring over a medium heat until dissolved and then cook until caramelised to golden brown. Remove and stir in the nuts, tip onto a heatproof surface, silicone mat or non-stick baking parchment, leave to harden and cool. Pulse in a food processor until crumbly in texture.

For the mousse, reduce the beer and sugar by boiling carefully until it forms a syrupy texture. Remove from the heat. Soak the gelatine in cold water for 5 minutes. Drain the gelatine and whisk it into the beer syrup until dissolved. Sieve into cold bowl and allow to cool.

Whip the cream until thick and mix with mascarpone. Fold in the stout syrup. Whisk the egg whites until stiff peaks and fold gently but thoroughly.

Line six individual ring moulds with clingfilm and divide mousse between them.

To serve, remove the mousses carefully by removing from the moulds and peel off the clingfilm. Top with a sprinkling of praline and garnish with chocolate biscuits or shortbread. Best eaten with a glass of stout on the side.

An arts and crafts building in genteel Walberswick, The Anchor sits behind the village allotments overlooking the dunes and beach huts behind. An attractive seaside pub with rooms, gutsy fresh food and world class drinks, it has been created with parties and feasting in mind; heated flint barn and in-house cinema; six outside chalets and five bedrooms in house; rear terrace overlooking the beach with outside bar for barbecued fish and 'fruits de mer' platters on sunny weekends. Dining is the main attraction, ingredients well sourced and hearty food full of vibrant flavours - West Mersea oysters, Lowestoft smoked fish, Jimmy Butler's famous Blythburgh pork, Edward Turner's 'Seahawk' Red Poll beef, vegetables from local farms and our allotment. Bread is kneaded and baked daily. Wines are from pioneering growers – the likes of Huet, Ridge, Anne Gros and John Forrest – whilst superb beers are created by iconic brewers Sierra Nevada, Orval, Adnams and Meantime.
The Anchor, Main Street, Walberswick, Suffolk IP18 6UA
T: 01502 722112 W: www.anchoratwalberswick.com

Acknowledgements

In no particular order, so many people have been instrumental in creating **Pie in the Sky**:

All at the East Anglian Air Ambulance - the HQ team, especially Simon, Christine, Richard, Pip and Rebecca; the county fundraisers; and of course the many lovely volunteers, who, not only have been promoting the recipe competition and the book, but will also be key to selling thousands of copies to keep the helicopters flying.

The county judges of our EAAA's regional competition to find the winning public recipes for 'Pie in the Sky' - our own East Anglian celebrity chef Galton Blackiston of Morston Hall in north Norfolk; chef-patron Stephen David of The Crown at Woodbridge in east Suffolk; Jason Waterfield, Executive Head Chef of King's College, Cambridge University; and Martin Lee, chef-proprietor of The Plough at Bolnhurst in Bedfordshire. Particular thanks to both The Plough at Bolnhurst, Beds and to The Crown at Woodbridge, Suffolk, who so generously provided the EAAA with delightful lunch parties for our media launches in their excellent establishments. W: www.morstonhall.com www.thecrownatwoodbridge.co.uk www.kings.cam.ac.uk/venue www.bolnhurst.com

Luke, Chris and their brigade of chefs from The Crown at Woodbridge for preparing all the celebrity and public recipes. And Stephen, who as always has gone the extra mile, checking recipes, hosting meetings, food styling for photography and passionately believing in **Pie in the Sky**. W: www.thecrownatwoodbridge.co.uk

Peter Butler of Stepjump Design, Nayland who generously provided an excellent illustration for our book merchandising, interpreting our distinctly layman ideas. W: www.stepjumpdesign.com

Keiron Tovell, the very capable Norfolk based food photographer who superbly captured many of the recipe images. W: www.keirontovell.com

Chris Grover, the talented Suffolk wedding photographer who generously interrupted his holiday in the French sun to help us. W: www.fotonovo.com

The ever-patient and gifted Mark, Simon, and Kelly of *season* magazine at BC Publications for putting up with all the frustrations of a last minute project and doing a wonderful job in designing the book, completely for free. W: www.seasonmagazine.co.uk

Beryl and Idris Williams for their editorial eye and liberal use of red ink in proof-reading the manuscript.

The enthusiastic James Robinson and all the helpful Fuller Davies team and suppliers who printed the book in record time and reduced their bill to a more than charitable price. W: www.fullerdavies.com and their able suppliers – Lamination by Coatings Direct of Bury St.Edmunds. W: www.olrogroup.co.uk – Burst Binding by Diamond Print Services. W: www.diamondprintservices.co.uk – Paper supplied by Masons Paper of Ipswich. W: www.paperco.co.uk

Tony and all his team at Tastes of Anglia Table, the local food and drink specialists, for helping us distribute the book. W: www.tastesofanglia.com

And finally, last but definitely not least, a huge thank you to all the celebrities, local chefs and you, the great East Anglian public, for giving us all these wonderful recipes, it really has made **Pie in the Sky** a pleasure to produce.

Index

PICTURE CREDITS

Cover: images supplied; by Keiron Tovell; from istockphoto.com
Foreword: page 5 supplied
Intro: page 6 by Keiron Tovell; page 9 courtesy / copyright of Elliot Macrow
East Anglian Air Ambulance: page 10 and 11 supplied
The Celebrities: supplied except: page 24 courtesy / copyright of Eastern Daily Press (Archant Norfolk);
pages 14, 18 and 25 by Keiron Tovell
The Great East Anglian Public: pages 28 to 44 by Keiron Tovell
The Local Chefs: supplied except: page 48 by Keiron Tovell
Keiron Tovell is available for photographic commissions via W: www.keirontovell.com

DERBYSHII
LOST VILLAGES
WALKS

BY
JOHN N. MERRILL

" I hike the paths and trails of the world for others to enjoy."

Maps, photographs and sketches by John N. Merrill.

2001

Walk & Write Ltd.

Walk & Write Ltd.,
Unit 1, Molyneux Business Park,
Whitworth Road, Darley Dale,
Derbyshire, England. DE4 2HJ

Tel/Fax 01629 - 735911

email- marathonhiker@aol.com
WWW - members.aol.com:/marathonhiker

PUBLISHED BY - WALK & WRITE LTD.
TYPSET AND DESIGNED BY JOHN MERRILL/WALK & WRITE LTD.
PRINTED BY BOOTS & BOOKS.

© TEXT - JOHN N. MERRILL. 2001
© MAPS, SKETCHES AND PHOTOGRAPHS BY JOHN N. MERRILL. 2001

ISBN 1-903627-09-5
FIRST PUBLISHED - MARCH 2001

BRITISH LIBRARY CATALOGUING-IN-PUBLICATION DATA. A CATALOGUE RECORD OF THIS BOOK IS AVAILABLE FROM THE BRITISH LIBRARY.

TYPESET BY JOHN MERRILL, IN BOOKMAN- BOLD, ITALIC, AND PLAIN 10PT, 14PT AND 18PT .

PLEASE NOTE - THE MAPS IN THIS GUIDE ARE PURELY ILLUSTRATIVE. YOU ARE ENCOURAGED TO USE THE APPROPRIATE 1:25,000 O.S. MAP.

JOHN N. MERRILL HAS WALKED ALL THE ROUTES IN THIS BOOK. METICULOUS RESEARCH HAS BEEN UNDERTAKEN TO ENSURE THAT THIS PUBLICATION IS HIGHLY ACCURATE AT THE TIME OF GOING TO PRESS. THE PUBLISHERS, HOWEVER, CANNOT BE HELD RESPONSIBLE FOR ALTERATIONS, ERRORS, OMISSIONS, OR FOR CHANGES IN DETAILS GIVEN. THEY WOULD WELCOME INFORMATION TO HELP KEEP THE BOOK UP TO DATE.

COVER DESIGN - BY JOHN N. MERRILL - WALK & WRITE LTD © 2001
PHOTGGRAPH - "MAIN STREET, HUNGEY BENTLEY" BY JOHN N. MERRILL

About John N. Merrill

Few people have walked the earth's crust more than John Merrill with more than 170000 miles in the last 30 years - the average person walks 75,000 miles in a lifetime. Apart from walking too much causing bones in his feet to snap, like metal fatigue, he has never suffered from any back, hip or knee problems. Like other walkers he has suffered from many blisters, his record is 23 on both feet! He wears out at least three pairs of boots a year and his major walking has cost over £125,000. This includes 91 pairs of boots costing more than £10,500 and over £1,500 on socks - a pair of socks last three weeks and are not washed.

His marathon walks in Britain include - -

Hebridean Journey....... 1,003 miles. Northern Isles Journey......913 miles.
Irish Island Journey ....1,578 miles.   Parkland Journey.......2,043 miles.
Land's End to John o' Groats.....1,608 miles.

and in 1978 he became the first person to walk the entire coastline of Britain - 6,824 miles in ten months.

In Europe he has walked across Austria - 712 miles - hiked the Tour of Mont Blanc, the Normandy coast, the Loire Valley (450 miles), a high level route across the Augverne(230 miles) and the River Seine (200 miles) in France, completed High Level Routes in the Dolomites and Italian Alps, and the GR20 route across Corsica in training! Climbed the Tatra Mountains ,the Transylvanian Alps in Romania, and in Germany walked in the Taunus, Rhine, the Black Forest (Clock Carriers Way) and King Ludwig Way (Bavaria). He has walked across Europe - 2,806 miles in 107 days - crossing seven countries, the Swiss and French Alps and the complete Pyrennean chain - the hardest and longest mountain walk in Europe, with more than 600,000 feet of ascent! He has walked 1,100 miles along the pilgrimage route from Le Puy (France) to Santiago (Spain) and onto Cape Finisterre. In the autumn of 2,000 he walked 270 miles from Prague to Vienna, across the Czech Republic.

In America he used The Appalachian Trail - 2,200 miles - as a training walk, before walking from Mexico to Canada via the Pacific Crest Trail in record time - 118 days for 2,700 miles. Recently he walked most of the Continental Divide Trail and much of New Mexico; his second home. He has walked the Chesopeake & Ohio Canal National Historical Trail and in 2000, 1,310 miles in Ohio, following The Buckeye Trail. In Canada he has walked the Rideau Trail - Kingston to Ottawa - 220 miles and The Bruce Trail - Tobermory to Niagara Falls - 460 miles.

In 1984 John set off from Virginia Beach on the Atlantic coast, and walked 4,226 miles without a rest day, across the width of America from Cape Henry, Virginia to Santa Cruz and San Francisco on the Pacific coast. His walk was the longest ,and hardest crossing of the U.S.A. in the shortest time - under six months (178 days). The direct distance is 2,800 miles.

Between major walks John is out training in his own area - The Peak District National Park. He has walked all of our National Trails many times - The Cleveland Way thirteen times and The Pennine Way four times in a year! He has been trekking in the Himalayas five times. He created more than forty challenge walks which have been used to raise more than £600,000 for charity. From his own walks he has raised over £100,000. He is author of more than 200 walking guides which he prints and publishes himself, His book sales are in excess of 3 million, He has created many long distance walks including The Limey Way, The Peakland Way, Dark Peak Challenge walk, Rivers' Way, The Belvoir Witches Challenge Walk and the Forest of Bowland Challenge.

CONTENTS

4

INTRODUCTION

The Peak District and Derbyshire are littered with hundreds of lost village sites, abandoned for a wide variety of reasons over the centuries. This collection of walks take you many of the more outstanding examples and are fascinating historical walks. Not only to see where history was made but also explore fully an area and its variety of historical features. Some of the walks maybe in familiar terrain but, I suspect like me, you walked along the path unaware that a village existed in the next field! The selection of walks bring you to most of the types of "lost Village."

Some of the types of lost villages through the ages are -

a. Prehistoric - such as hill forts - Mam Tor and Carl Wark.

b. Roman - forts such as Navio (Brough) and Derventio (Derby).

c. Sheep clearances by Monastic landlords. Derbyshire is littered, Granges - meaning associated with an Abbey. Wool was a very important commodity of English Medieval trade - to Flanders and Italy - and great profits were made by the church. Such as Roystone Grange, Conksbury and Ingleby. The Lord Chancellor still sits on a woolsack.

d. Climatic changes - due to changes it was no longer possible to support the village from the dry earth - such as Hungry Bentley.

e. The Black Death 1345/6 - Devastated Derbyshire and many villages were abandoned - such as Steetley.

f. Ruthless landlords who moved the village out of their view! - such as at Chatsworth (Edensor), Foremark and Longford.

g. Submerged villages, removed to allow valleys to be flooded for reservoirs - such as Derwent and Ashopton.

The walks, for me have been a never ending venture of discovery. Looking in the churches and discovering their past or where the font came from. Seeing at first hand the house mounds and streets of a mediaeval village. Then going the library to research and learn more about what I had see on the ground. Visiting museums and seeing finds uncovered from a specific site. Whilst the walks are now completed the discovery and adventure continues. I hope you enjoy these historical walks and learn more about area.

Happy walking! John N. Merrill

DERWENT AND ASHOPTON
- 11 MILES

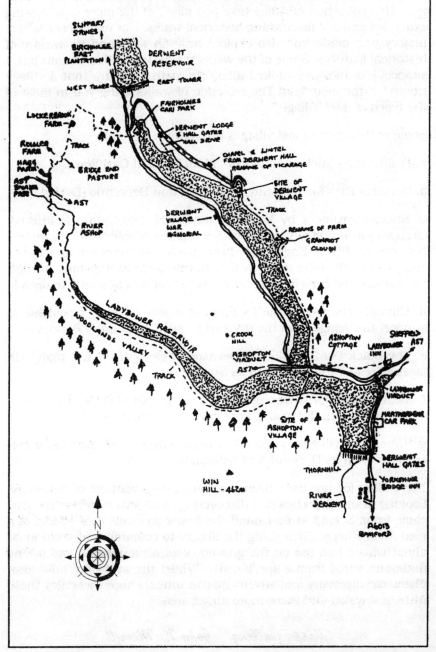

SLIPPERY STONES

BIRCHINLEE EAST PLANTATION

DERWENT RESERVOIR

WEST TOWER

EAST TOWER

FAIRHOLMES CAR PARK

LOCKERBROOK FARM

DERWENT LODGE & HALL GATES

HALL DRIVE

ROWLEE FARM

TRACK

CHAPEL & LINTEL FROM DERWENT HALL

REMAINS OF VICARAGE

HAGG FARM

BRIDGE END PASTURE

SITE OF DERWENT VILLAGE

A57 SNAKE PASS

A57

RIVER ASHOP

DERWENT VILLAGE WAR MEMORIAL

TRACK

REMAINS OF FARM

GRAINFOOT CLOUGH

LADYBOWER RESERVOIR

WOODLANDS VALLEY

CROOK HILL

ASHOPTON COTTAGE

SHEFFIELD

LADYBOWER INN

A57

ASHOPTON VIADUCT

A57

TRACK

LADYBOWER VIADUCT

HEATHERDENE CAR PARK

SITE OF ASHOPTON VILLAGE

DERWENT HALL GATES

THORNHILL

YORKSHIRE BRIDGE INN

WIN HILL - 462m

RIVER DERWENT

A6013 BAMFORD

N

DERWENT AND ASHOPTON
- 11 MILES
- allow 4 to 5 hours

Route - Heatherdene Car Park - Ladybower Reservoir Dam Wall - Woodlands Valley - River Ashop - Haggwater Bridge - A57 - Hagg Farm - Lockerbrook Farm - Fairholmes Car Park - River Derwent - Derwent - Ladybower Reservoir - Ashopton - Ladybower Inn - A57 - A6013 - Heatherdene Car Park.

Map - 1:25,000 Outdoor Leisure map No. 1 - The Dark Peak - East Sheet.

Car Park - Heatherdene. Beside A6013, overlooking Ladybower Reservoir, southern end. Severn Trent Water Board facility with toilets. Grid Ref. SK204858.

Inns - Ladybower Inn.

Teas - Fairholmes Car park. Derwent Lodge.

ABOUT THE WALK - Simply fascinating! Basically you encircle Ladybower Reservoir, which was opened in 1945. The two flooded valleys submerged two villages - Ashopton and Derwent. The former lies underneath Ashopton Viaduct with only a few houses above the waterline, which you pass. Derwent likewise only a few of the upper village remains. However you can still see the hall gates of Derwent Hall and its lodge, plus a lintel. If time permits a visit to Bamford church completes the story. Much of the walk is level walking with an ascent from the River Ashop to the River Derwent at the halfway point. The walk is all the more fascinating following the waterboard's Millennium project on the reservoir, costing 23 million pounds, has resulted in a path across the dam wall.

WALKING INSTRUCTIONS - In the car park lower level, turn left, as footpath signed - Ladybower Dam - and follow the path past the toilets to above the dam wall. Turn right and descend to the A6013 and dam wall. The gate pillars came from Derwent Hall. Cross the road and onto the dam wall - 1,250 ft. long - and walk along it to its end. Below, left, are the two tailgates from the reservoir. While a little further is the Yorkshire Bridge Inn and houses where the people from Ashopton and Derwent were rehoused. At the end of the dam wall turn right onto a tarmaced surface and walk above the reservoir. This soon turns left and becomes a track and for the next three miles follow it westwards above the reservoir with views to Ladybower and Ashopton Viaducts. Where the track turns right to a bridge over the River Ashop; 1/4 mile beyond the end of the reservoir, keep left on a gently ascending track. In less than 1/4 mile gain a stile and junction of a track on your right. Turn right and descend the track which soon levels out and in 1/4 mile brings you to a bridge - Haggwater Bridge - over the River Ashop and footpath sign - Snake Road. Cross and ascend the track to the Snake Road, A57.

Cross to your left and ascend the drive of Hagg Farm and where it turns left to it, keep straight ahead on a track. Follow its zig-zags to a gate and onto a crossroads of bridle paths. Keep straight ahead on a track - bridlepath sign - Lockerbrook - and gently descend to Lockerbrook farm. Continue on the track ascending gently for another 200 yards to a path sign on your right - Fairholmes. Turn right and descend the field by a wall on your left to a stile and pine forest. Follow the defined path as it zig-zag downs. Cross two tracks; basically keep straight ahead as you descend. As you near the road and Fairholmes Car Park pass the remains of the railway line used for the construction of Howden and Derwent Reservoirs in the early 1900's. Cross the road to your right to follow the tarmaced path around the edge of the car park. Soon it turns left, westwards, to the road beneath Derwent Reservoir dam wall. Keep right along it - on your left is a path to the west tower where there is a museum and display to the Dambusters and history of the Derwent Valley. Follow the road round to your right and in 1/4 mile pass Derwent Lodge and hall gates on your right. A few yards later on your left is Old House Farm (National Trust). More than 1/4 mile later pass a chapel end of a building. Ascend the steps to your left to see the lintel from Derwent Hall.

Continue on the road which soon curves left with the remains of Derwent Vicarage on your right. Walk around the small inlet to a notice board depicting the layout of the submerged Derwent village. The road now becomes a track as you continue above the reservoir and in 1/2 mile reach another small inlet - Grainfoot Clough - and on your right can be seen the remains of the farm here. Continue on the track for another mile to almost the A57 road with Ashopton Viaduct on your right. Before the road turn left and ascend past Ashopton Cottage and a little further to a gate and Ding Bank Farm. Continue ahead ascending the track a little further to where it turns left. Here on the right is a gate and path to Ladybower Inn. Keep the wall on your right as the path contours round and in 1/4 mile pass the inn on your right and just after reach a track on your right and turn right descending to the A57 road and Inn. Descend the road to the junction with the A6013 road and turn left along it over Ladybower Reservoir - Ladybower House is to your right. Follow the road round to the car park entrance and turn left into it.

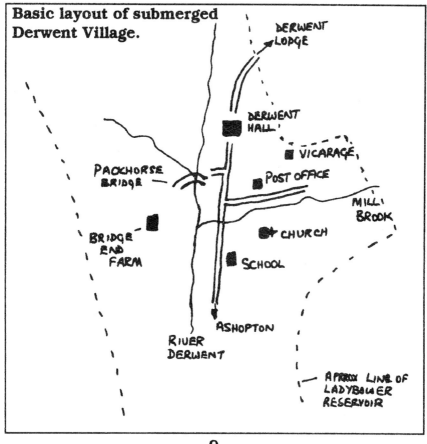

Basic layout of submerged Derwent Village.

9

J.B. Firth's book - *"Highways & Byways in Derbyshire"* (1928), records what the villages were like before being submerged.

Ashopton was at the junction of four valleys. "Ashopton itself consists of an inn and a few scattered houses - the inn, which was built for the convenience of passengers on the coach road by a considerate Duke of Devonshire, now being a favourite *terminus ad quem* for driving parties from Sheffield and the little towns of the Peak."

"One short excursion from Ashopton should in no wise be missed..... It is a short two miles up to the village of Derwent, where a beautiful two-arched bridge spans the river, flagged with stones like a pavement and much to narrow to admit the passage of any vehicle. This is an ancient packhorse bridge.........Nor is it an ordinary bridge clumsily put together.........at the first glance suggests ecclesiastical influence. So it proves. The White Canons of Welbeck (Dukeries) had great estates in Derwent Dale........Nearby stands Derwent Hall, one of the county seats of the Duke of Norfolk, an exquisite old house of many gables, surrounded by lovely gardens and set in the richest corner of this secluded valley.

LADYBOWER RESERVOIR - took eleven years to build and was officially opened by George V1 on September 25th 1945. You see the plaques before crossing the A57 to the dam wall. The reservoir has a holding capacity of 6.1 billion gallons.

Derwent Hall gate posts at entrance to Ladybower Reservoir Dam wall.

*Packhorse Bridge, near Derwent Hall. Sketch by Nelly Erichsen.
Taken from J.B.Firth's "Highways & Byways in Derbyshire."*

DERWENT HALL - was built by Henry Balguy in 1672. Later it became a shooting lodge of the Duke of Norfolk and in 1920 a Youth Hostel until it was demolished together with village in 1943.

DERWENT - The church tower was left standing but became a hazard as people swam out to it. It was blown up in 1946. The packhorse bridge was carefully dismantled and rebuilt beyond Howden Reservoir at Slippery Stones. Derwent village war memorial was repositioned on the otherside of the valley at SK182884 and basically overlooks the spot where it originally stood. The people in the churchyard were exhumed and reburied in Bamford churchyard. Entering the gate in the far righthand corner can be found the tombs; particularly noticeable are ones from the owners of Bridge End Farm. Path signs east of Ladybower Inn, dated 1933, still point to the village of Derwent.

BIRCHENLEE- This is a rare occurrence when a special village was built near Howden Reservoir at SK167915 and marked on the map. Roads and outline of buildings remain. The village, known as Tin Town, was occupied from 1901 to 1914. With Howden and Derwent complete it was demolished. Amongst the Derwent village tombs in Bamford churchyard can be seen a cross to the women. children and workers of Birchenlee who died while there.

CALTON, EDENSOR AND CHATSWORTH - 4 MILES

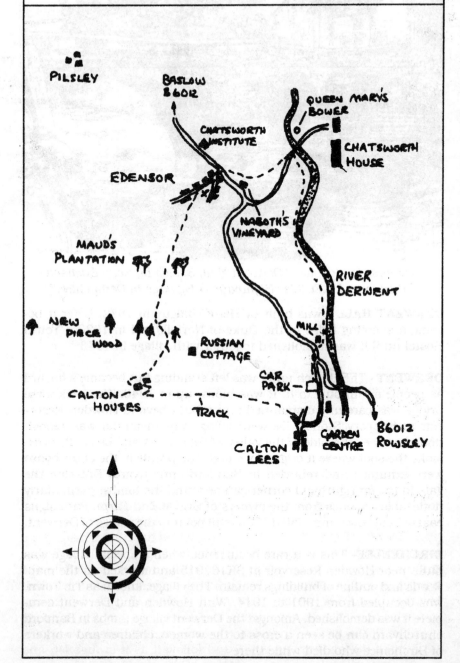

PILSLEY

BASLOW B6012

CHATSWORTH INSTITUTE

QUEEN MARY'S BOWER

CHATSWORTH HOUSE

EDENSOR

NABOTH'S VINEYARD

MAUD'S PLANTATION

RIVER DERWENT

NEW PIECE WOOD

MILL

RUSSIAN COTTAGE

CAR PARK

CALTON HOUSES

TRACK

GARDEN CENTRE

CALTON LEES

B6012 ROWSLEY

N

CALTON, EDENSOR, AND CHATSWORTH
- 4 MILES
- allow 2 hours.

 Route - Calton Lees Car park - Calton Houses - New Piece Wood - Edensor - River Derwent - Corn Mill - Calton Lees.

 Map - 1:25,000 Outdoor leisure Map No. 24 - The White Peak - East Sheet.

 Car Park - Calton Lees.

 Teas - Edensor Post Office. Chatsworth Garden Centre, Calton Lees.

Ice cream - Edensor Post Office. Kiosk opposite Calton Lees Car Park.

ABOUT THE WALK - Chatsworth House lies in an exceptional setting of beautiful parkland by a flowing river. But, as this walk demonstrates two villages were removed to create today's scene, by the Dukes of Devonshire. This walk takes you past the "village" of Calton (Grid Ref. SK685245), once the seat of the Calton family in the 14th century; later cleared. Then you descend to the present village of Edensor before passing the last surviving house in its original position before gaining the River Derwent and site of Chatsworth village.

WALKING INSTRUCTIONS - Turn right out of the car park along the road past the Chatsworth Garden Centre towards Calton Lees. Follow the road round to your right and where it turns sharp left to the hamlet, bear right along the level track by a stream on your left. Follow the track for more than 1/2 mile to Calton Houses and zig-zag upto the houses. On your right can be seen evidence of a house platform.Follow the ascending track between the houses to a gate. Bear right still on a grassy track and follow it as it swings left and

13

aiming for a stile and New Piece Wood. To your right on the edge of the wood can be seen Russian Cottage. Follow the track through and down, New Piece Wood, to a stile. Over this emerge into Chatsworth Park and descend gently aiming for the righthand side of an oval plantation with another, Maud's Plantation to your left. The church spire of Edensor acts as your guide, as you aim to the left of it, to gain a kissing gate and steps down into the village, more than 1/2 mile from New Piece Wood. Descend and turn right to the green and left to the road; after exploring the church and village. Cross the road and follow the defined path towards Chatsworth House, passing above "Naboth's Vineyard", the sole remaining house of the original village of Edensor. Follow the path to the bridge over the River Derwent. Turn right before it to walk close to the river for the final mile back to Calton Lees Car park. On the otherside of the bridge, on the left is Queen Mary's Bower. Keep the river on your left to the ruins of Chatsworth's Corn mill, still complete with gears and wheels and mill channel. It was used until the 1950"s. Turn right and ascend to the road and turn left back into the car park.

EDENSOR - An agricultural settlement was recorded close to the bank of the River Derwent, known as Edensoure, at the time of the Domesday Book.

"In Edensor Leofnoth and Ketel had 2 c. of land as two manors.
Henry how (has) 4 c. taxable and as many c. for ploughing.
10 villagers and 7 smallholders with 6 ploughs.
Meadow, 1 acre.
Value formerly 40s (£2); now 20s (£1)."

During the early work on the Elizabethan Chatsworth House, to the present building, the fourth Duke of Devonshire had part of Edensor village removed. Some moved into the remaining part of the village, while others moved to Pilsley, which was created for this purpose. The modification and enlargement of Chatsworth House, meant that the focal point of the house changed. Originally, the front was on the east side with the gardens rising up the slope. The 6th Duke of Devonshire, made the west front, facing the river, the front meaning that Edensor village came into his view. This included the Manor House, dated 1241. The duke in 1839/40 had the village removed to its present site, creating an uninterrupted view from the house. The present village is one of the finest model villages in Britain and was largely designed by Joseph Paxton. The houses are a mixture of architectural designs and include Gothic, Tudor, Renaissance, Swiss and Italianate styles. On the left of the Green is a Swiss style house, formerly the villagers alehouse. Both Paxton and several of the Dukes of Devon

-shire are buried in Edensor churchyard.

Naboth's Vineyard.

Only one house remains in its original position, Naboth's Vineyard (Grid Ref. SK253698), on the otherside of the road. The owner is reputedly either refused to sell to the Duke or that he was well liked by the Duke and allowed to stay. In front of the house runs the original High Street of the village. To its right can be seen a houses platform. Further traces of the village, occupied until 1838, can be seen in grass close to the junction of the house road and Baslow/Rowsley road. The only other survivor of the village is the present Chatsworth Institute. This is the former Edensor Inn. Boswell in 1775 visited the inn and wrote, "It had only recently been built."

CHATSWORTH - Grid Ref. SK2670. The house is built on the site of Chatsworth village, originally a monastic grange. On the righthand side (south-west) of the bridge over the River Derwent can be seen the outline of a moated site, Grid Ref SK257702. It has been suggested that this is the site of Chatsworth Manor.

The Domesday Book records -

> " In 'Langley' and Chatsworth Leofnoth and Ketel had 10 b. pf
> land taxable. Land for 10 oxen. It lies in Edensor (lands).
> William Peveril has charge for the King.
> 5 villagers and 2 smallholders have 2 ploughs.
> Meadow, 1 acre; woodland pasture 1 league long
> and 1 wide; a little underwood.
> Value before 1066, 20s (£1); now 16s (80p)."

15

CONKSBURY - 3 MILES

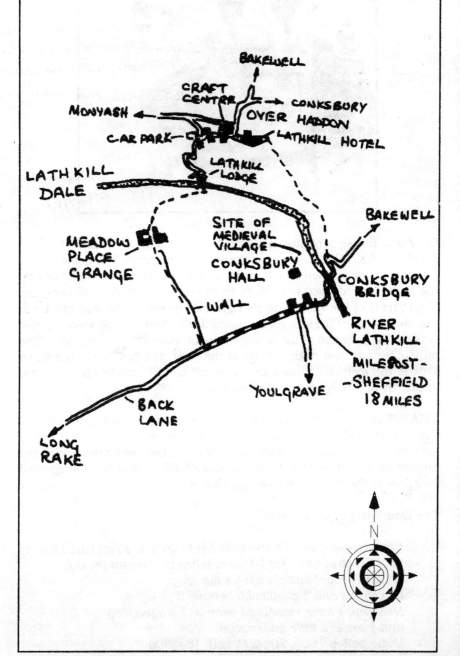

CONKSBURY
- 3 MILES
- allow 2 hours

Route - Over Haddon - Conksbury Bridge - Meadow Place Grange - Lathkill Lodge - Over Haddon.

Map - 1:25,000 Outdoor Leisure Map No. 24 - The White Peak - East Sheet.

Car Park - Over Haddon.

Inns - Lathkill Hotel, Over Haddon.

Teas - Conksbury Farm (Outside seating only). Yew Tree Cafe and Geoff's Diner ; Over Haddon.

ABOUT THE WALK - One of only two *"site of Mediaeval Village"* marked on the O.S. White Peak map - Gratton is the other; see Middleton walk. The site close to Conksbury Hall - Grid Ref. SK208657 - is on private land and has little to be seen. You have a good view of the location as you descend above Lathkill Dale to Conksbury Bridge. There is evidence of house platforms. Conksbury Bridge is a favourite vantage point for admiring the view to Over Haddon and to gaze at the clear waters of the River Lathkill; the clearest in England. The bridge, Grid Ref. SK212655, was used as a sheepwash- for washing the sheep prior to shearing - was used until 1950. Meadow Place Grange, Grid Ref. SK201658, which was associated with Augustinian, Leicester Abbey, is the site of a monastic clearance. This is a short hilly route with much to see.

WALKING INSTRUCTIONS - From the car park turn right to the Yew Tree Tearoom and road junction. Turn left - the descending road to your right is your return path! Follow the road and where it forks keep left and descend the narrow lane to the village well pump and onto the Lathkill Hotel. At the road bend beside the inn go through a stile and keep to the righthand path and cross the field to a stile. Continue descending to another on the edge of Lathkill Dale. Bear left along its edge with impressive views west and east along the dale. Opposite and above Conksbury Bridge can be seen Conksbury Hall close to the site of the Mediaeval Village. Continue on the path and turn right to descend to the sharp bend in the road from Conksbury, emerging via a stile into a small parking area. Descend the road and cross Conksbury Bridge. Follow the road round to your right to a farm on your right - teas - and an old milepost - Sheffield 18 miles - at the end of a wall. Keep on the road for 1/4 mile, (ignoring the turning left to Youlgreave), to a path sign and stile on your right. Over the stile keep the wall on your right to a stile as Meadow Place Grange comes into view. Descend first by the wall then slightly left to a path sign and gate into the farm yard. Go straight across, as signed to another gate. Keep ahead in the field bearing slightly right over the "brow" to a gate in the far righthand corner. Turn right through the gate and descend a track in woodland and follow it round to your left to the slab bridge over the River Lathkill opposite Lathkill Lodge. Cross and gain the lane and ascend steeply the zig-zag road back to Yew Tree Cafe, Car Park and Over Haddon.

CONKSBURY - At the time of the Domesday Book, Conksbury spelt - "Conkesbury" was an outliner of Bakewell Manor.

William Avenel gave to the Abbey of Leicester, Meadow Place Grange and its land together with the hamlet of Conksbury with its water mill and 20 acres of land in Over Haddon.

Conksbury Bridge is Medieval and was once part of the road from Bakewell to Newhaven. The bridge is believed to have been built by the monks and is first documented in 1296.

Conksbury Mill was located further down the dale. A dispute is recorded in the Close Rolls dated May 10, 1344, when the Abbot of Leicester accused 15 local men of *"having broken the ponds and sluices of the Abbot's mills at Congisbury."* The outcome is not knowm.

MEADOW PLACE GRANGE - Belonged to the Abbey of Leicester, which was founded in 1143 AD; The Augustinian order of Our Lady of the Meadows. The Grange land consisted of 731 acres. At the time of the Dissolution in 1536 (Henry VIII) the value of the Grange was - £22. 13s. 4d (£22.66p) per annum. Attached to the Grange was an ancient chapel which was demolished in October 1856. A drawing made by Thomas Bateman just before it was destroyed, shows it having a Norman doorway.

MIDDLETON AND GRATTON
- 10 MILES

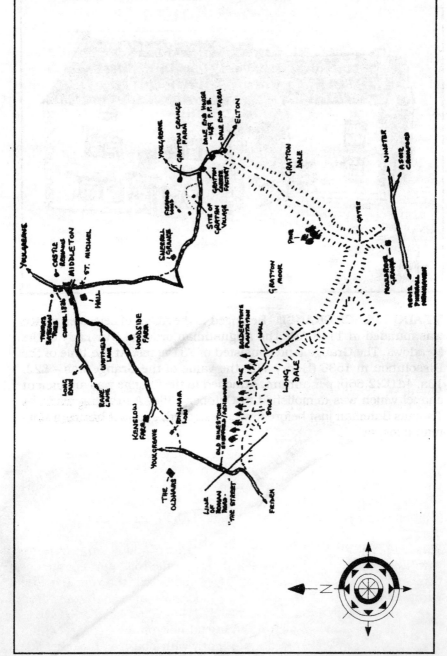

MIDDLETON AND GRATTON
- 10 MILES
- allow 4 hours

Route - Middleton - Whitfield Lane - Ringham Low - Line of "The Street" Roman Road - Long Dale - Mouldridge Grange - Gratton dale - Dale End - Site of Gratton Village - Smerrill Grange - Middleton.

Map - 1:25,000 Outdoor leisure Map No. 24 - The White Peak - East Sheet.

VISITOR PARKING

Car park - Roadside parking in Middleton.

Inns - None carry what you need.

ABOUT THE WALK - A stunning walk through two quiet dales in an area rich in Monastic sheep farming. Middleton is worth exploring at the end to see the site of Fulwood Castle and Thomas Bateman's tomb. First you cross the limestone plateau to pass close to prehistoric burial chamber, Ringham Low. You descend gently to Long Dale passing an old milepost and line of the Roman Road - The Street. Next you walk through the quite and dry Long Dale to its junction with Gratton Dale. A side trip gives you close views of Mouldridge Grange, before walking through Gratton Dale and old limekiln to Dale End. Soon afterwards you pass the former Gratton Cheese Factory and just after the site of Gratton village - marked *"Medieval Village (site of)"* on the map. A short distance later you pass Smerrill Grange before walking back into Middleton, passing its small church and Middleton Hall.

WALKING INSTRUCTIONS - From the centre of Middleton turn right, with the play area on your left, and ascend the road passing the entrance to Middleton Hall and later The Pinfold (road) on your left. 200 yards later turn left onto a tarmaced lane, unnamed but named on the map - Whitfield Lane. In more than 1/4 mile pass the entrance to Woodside Farm on your left. Keep ahead now on a walled track and more than 1/4 mile later, descend slightly with a barn on the otherside

21

Old milepost near "The Street".

of the dale and a dew pond on your left. Keep on the track as it curves right here and a further 1/4 mile where the track turns right to Kenslow Farm at a gate, bear diagonally left, as path signed - Friden, and cross the field to a gap and onto a stile. Continue to another and to your right over the wall in field corner is the small circular mound of Ringham Low; on a vantage point. Cross the field to a track and cross via stiles and continue across the next field to a stile, pathsign and Friden/Newhaven road. Turn left along it passing the entrance to The Oldhams Farm. 1/4 mile later as you descend towards Long dale on your left can be seen an old milepost with the words Sheffield and Ashbourne just decipherable. Follow the road round to your right then left, crossing the line of the Roman Road, "The Street".

Round the otherside turn left onto a path to a gate and continue along a walled path into Long Dale. At the end of the wall keep ahead along the dale floor to a stile. Keep the wall and wood on your left to its end and stile. Turn left and ascend the dale side to a gate on its edge on the right. Turn right and continue on the path above the dale keeping a wall on your left at first. This soon turns left to a corner, but you keep ahead on the path with views of the dale. The wall soon rejoins you and at a gate on your left, where a track, "The Peakway" crosses to near Smerrill Grange, bear right slightly and soon descend to the dale floor and a small gate. Continue along the floor of the dale for a mile to a gate and junction with Gratton Dale. Before turning left down this dale, turn right and ascend the path to see Mouldridge Grange. Return to the dale junction and turn right through another gate and follow the defined path through Gratton Dale. Keep to the dale floor and after nearly 1 1/2 miles reach a gate with a limekiln on your left. Continue ahead to a stile and pathsign and gain Dale End, and road to Elton.

Turn left and pass Dale End House with date stone P.P.B. 1689. Soon afterwards at the road junction pass the former, Gratton Cheese Factory, on your left. Keep to the lefthand road and start gently ascending. As you do so on your right can be seen the site of Gratton Village and house platforms can be seen. On the otherside is Gratton Grange Farm and Fishpond Wood. Continue on the narrow lane and in 1/2 mile pass Smerrill Grange on your right. Just after turn right at a gate and path sign. Walk beside the wall on your right to the second stile. Go through this and continue descending to your right, steeply at the end to a stile and regain the road; having cut the corner off. Turn right walking along "Weaddow Lane" and half a mile later pass Middleton Hall on your left and St. Michael's Church on your right and regain central Middleton with the play area and Wellington Bomber plaque on your left - see my book, "White Peak Wreck Walks." If you walk towards Youlgreave a little way you can see the Fulwood Castle site on your right and just past Chapel Cottage - chapel dated 1826 - turn left along a signed path - Bateman's Tomb - and visit his tomb.

MIDDLETON - At the time of the Domesday Book, Middleton was an Outliner of the Manor of Wirksworth. Middleton church, dedicated to St. Michael was opened on 15th June 1865...."but has since been closed since that time" - recorded in Blacks Tourist Guide to Derbyshire, 1879. The building was restored in 1899. William and Thomas Bateman - see tomb notes - brought water to the village and their initials can be seen on the old wells. The village once had an inn known as Bateman's Arms.

MIDDLETON GRANGE - In 1152 the Squire of Youlgreave gave Youlgreave church and chapels including Middleton and Gratton to the Augustian Abbey of St. Mary. Leicester, founded in 1143AD. They established several Granges including Gratton Grange. Henry 11 bestowed Middleton Chapel on the Abbey. In the grounds of Middleton Hall in the 19th century, a vaulted passageway and foundations of the Grange were discovered.

RINGHAM LOW - Chambered Neolithic tomb, now largely destroyed, but the small round mound can still be seen. Excavations revealed four burial chambers with 18 skeletons.

23

ROMAN ROAD - "The Street" - ran from Little Chester (Derby) to Buxton.

MOULDRIDGE GRANGE - Linear enclosures and remains of buildings. Held by Dunstable Priory.

GRATTON CHEESE FACTORY - Run by the Gratton Dairy Co - Cheese Factors. In 1912 it is recorded - "Turning out about 3,000 cheeses annually."

GRATTON - The Domesday Book records - *"In Gratton Ketel had 1 c. of land taxable. Land for 2 ploughs. Now in Lordship 1 plough. 4 villages and 2 smallholders have 2 ploughs.*
Meadow, 3 acres.
Value before 1066, 10s (50p)."

House mounds can be seen in the field with the present day Gratton Grange Farm opposite. To its left is Fishpond Wood, indicating that the monks breed fish here for their table.

SMERRILL GRANGE - Monastic. Note mullioned windows on the lefthand side of the building. In 1846 recorded as - "Consists of one farm, the property of the Duke of Rutland. The whole is tithe-free."

THOMAS BATEMAN TOMB - William (father) and Thomas (son) excavated extensively in Derbyshire and elsewhere. Their finds were kept and displayed at Lomberdale House on the outskirts of the village. A 305 page book of the fields was published in 1885 - "A Descriptive catalogue of the Antiquities and Miscelleanous Objects, preserved in the Museum of Thomas Bateman at Lomberdale House." Thomas Bateman also wrote - "Vestiges of the Antiquities of Derbyshire" and "Ten years' Digging in Celtic Grave-mounds". The finds are now on display in the Sheffield Museum (Weston Park). Thomas Bateman's tomb is reached via a path on the right of the former Congregational Chapel built by Thomas Bateman in 1826. His tomb, which also includes his wife, has a stone model at the front of a Bronze Age Cinerary Urn.

FULWOOD CASTLE - Built by the Fulwood family and in the 17th century, Sir Christopher Fulwood was an ardent Royalist of Charles 1. During the Civil War he was able to muster 1,000 men for the cause. Unfortunately he was surprised by the Parliamentarians and fled to Bradfield Dale below. Here he was discovered behind a rock - now known as Fulwood's Rock - and was shot. The castle was destroyed and only one wall and mounds of its outline remain. Much of the stone was used to build Castle Farm adjacent to the site.

25

THE ROYSTONE GRANGE TRAIL
- 3 MILES

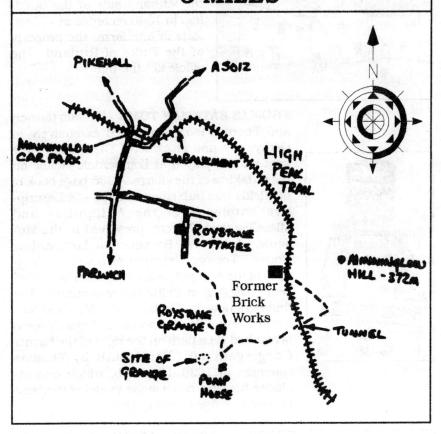

ROYSTONE GRANGE NOTES - The project to excavate the site was initated by Sheffield University in 1978. Their excavations revealed a Roman farm with field systems and remaining walls, together with the medieval Monastic sheep Grange. Finds from the excavations can be seen at the Sheffield Museum (Weston Park). These include flint tools - 5,000 - 300 BC; late Neolithic pottery; Bronze Age pottery and skulls from a barrow - 1800 - 1400 BC. From the medieval period a spindle whorl; pottery and iron objects. For a detailed account of the excavations see - *"Wall to Wall History - The Story of Roystone Grange"* by Richard Hodges. 1992.

THE ROYSTONE GRANGE TRAIL
- 3 MILES
- allow 1 1/2 hours.

Route - Minninglow Car Park (High Peak Trail) - Roystone Cottages - Roystone Grange - High Peak Trail - Minninglow Embankment - Minninglow Car park.

Map - 1:25,000 Outdoor Leisure Map - The White Peak - East Sheet.

Car Park - Minninglow Car Park on the High Peak Trail. Grid Ref. SK194883.

Inns & Tea rooms - None.

ABOUT THE WALK - A magnificent little trail steeped in history. The main feature is the site of Roystone Grange, which has been excavated, a former Monastic sheep farm during the 12th and 14th centuries. Only the outline of the buildings remain. The land was given by Adam of Harthill in the 12th century during the reign of Henry 11 - *"Pasture, beasts, apperantances in the vill of Revestones."* Roystone Grange was run by the Cistercian Abbey of Garendon, Leicestershire. Their other Granges were at Biggin and Heathcote. You return from the Grange area along the High Peak Trail at its most impressive along embankments and past the remains of a small quarry, The nearby Minninglow is the site of prehistoric burials.

WALKING INSTRUCTIONS - Return to the road from the car park and turn right and in a few yards left with Cobblersnook Plantation on your right. Walk along the lane to its end at a crossroads. Here turn left -there are infrequent yellow arrows with the initial R in the middle - on the route. Walk along the lane for 1/4 mile and turn right and descend past Roystone Cottages on your right. Continue ahead on a track following round to your left then right to a cattle grid and on todays Roystone Grange - some of the stone from the earlier one has been used in these buildings. Walk past the buildings and de

27

scend along the track and pass a stile and path sign on your left - this is your route - but first keep ahead to a chapel like building. This is was a 19th century pump house for the High Peak Trail. There is a plaque on the righthand side to Roystone Grange. Further right is the outline of the grange.

Retrace your steps back to the stile and path sign and turn right and cross the field to a stile. After this keep the wall on your left to a stile and then the wall is on your right. Ascend to a stile and on to a tunnel beneath the High Peak Railway. Walk through and keep straight ahead across the field to a stile and path sign. Over this gain a walled track and turn left and follow it to the High Peak Trail. Turn right along the trail - to your right is the wooded summit of Minninglow and burial chambers; on your left a former brick works. Walk along an embankment then a cutting and pass an old quarry and remains of a crane on your right. Keep on the trail for the next 3/4 mile walking along the Minninglow Embankment, which at over 600 feet long is the longest on the trail/railway line. Cross a minor road and enter the car park area where you began.

ROYSTONE GRANGE - A very important sheep Grange with 400 acres. During the 12th and 14th century wool from here was exported to Europe. During excavations between 1980-1987, the layout has been determined and the remains of a Roman house; some of the field walls date back to Roman times. The excavations revealed four building phases. Originally a three roomed building; then a separate more monastic building - an elegant hall - was built. Later the ground floors flooded leading to abandoning the site. Finds including pottery, a silver Edward 1st coin, a spinning whorl and iron tools, can be seen at Sheffield City Museum.

Site of Roystone Grange.

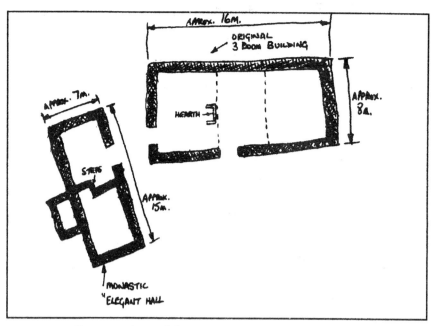

Basic outline of the monastic Roystone Grange.

The present Roystone Grange is 19th century and the barn has a door jam and lintel from the monastic building.

GREAT CUBLEY AND THREE MEDIEVAL LOST VILLAGES - 11 MILES

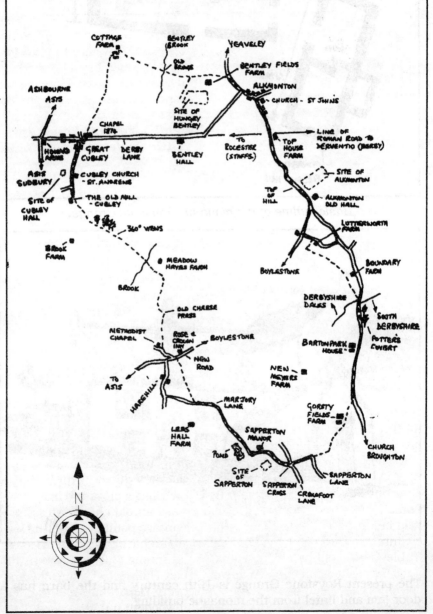

COTTAGE FARM

BENTLEY BROOK

OLD BRIDGE

YEAVELEY

BENTLEY FIELDS FARM

ALKMONTON

CHURCH - ST JOHNS

ASHBOURNE A515

CHAPEL 1874

SITE OF HUNGRY BENTLEY

HOWARD ARMS

GREAT CUBLEY

DERBY LANE

BENTLEY HALL

TO ROCESTER (STAFFS.)

TOP HOUSE FARM

LINE OF ROMAN ROAD TO DERVENTIO (DERBY)

A515 SUDBURY

CUBLEY CHURCH - ST. ANDREWS

THE OLD MILL - CUBLEY

TOP OF HILL

SITE OF ALKMONTON

ALKMONTON OLD HALL

SITE OF CUBLEY HALL

360° VIEWS

LOTTERWORTH FARM

BROOK FARM

MEADOW HAYES FARM

BOUNDARY FARM

BROOK

BOYLESTONE

DERBYSHIRE DALES

OLD CHEESE PRESS

SOUTH DERBYSHIRE

METHODIST CHAPEL

ROSE & CROWN INN

BOYLESTONE

BARTON PARK HOUSE

POTTER'S COVERT

NEW ROAD

NEW MEYERS FARM

TO A515

HAREHILL

MARJORY LANE

GORSTY FIELDS FARM

LEES HALL FARM

SAPPERTON MANOR

POND

CHURCH BROUGHTON

SITE OF SAPPERTON

SAPPERTON CROSS

SAPPERTON LANE

CROWFOOT LANE

N

GREAT CUBLEY AND THREE MEDIEVAL LOST VILLAGES
- 11 miles
- allow 5 to 6 hours.

Route - Great Cubley - Cubley Cottage Farm - Bentley Brook - Site of Hungry Bentley - Bentley Fields Farm - Alkmonton - Top House Farm - Site of Alkmonton - Alkmonton Old Hall - Littleworth farm - Potter's Covert - Bartonpark House - Gorsty Fields Farm - Sapperton Cross - Site of Sapperton - Sapperton Manor - Harehill - Meadow Hayes Farm - The Old Mill, Cubley - Little Cubley; church - Great Cubley.

Map- 1:25,000 Explorer Series No. 259 - Derby, Uttoxeter, Ashbourne & Cheadle.

Car Park - None. Limited roadside parking in Great Cubley.

Inn - Rose & Crown Inn, Harehill.

ABOUT THE WALK - Quiet simply; remarkable! Whilst longer than most in this book, the walk is so full of history that the miles float by while you explore the sites of three Medieval villages and much more. All three were deserted because of climatic change, resulting in poor produce from the land that the villagers were dependent upon. The old English word Hungry means - "poor or unproductive land". And Bentley means "bent-grass clearing." Not only do you explore these sites but also see a Norman font from one village; cross the line of the Roman Road from Derby to Rocester; pass an old cheese press in a field before ascending to a remarkable vantage point over South Derbyshire. And, to complete the historical/archaeological theme pass Cubley's old mill before reaching the stunning Cubley church. Finally, opposite is the moated site of Cubley Hall. Select a fine day and set off on one the finest walks of discovery Derbyshire has to offer. The paths are signed and well stiled (all wooden) but little used.

31

WALKING INSTRUCTIONS - From the cross roads in Great Cubley with the old village pump dated 1902 on the northern side, turn right along Derby Road, signposted Alkmonton. Pass the Village Hall on your right and a few yards later turn left onto a track beside a chapel dated 1874 - the footpath sign is well to the right! Walk past the chapel to a stile and keep the hedge on your left to the next one. Bear slightly right to the next before crossing the field to a hedge on your right. Keep the hedge on your right to a gate and continue ahead with the hedge now on your left. The path line now becomes a track as you approach the buildings of Cubley Cottage Farm. Turn right between them and left and after passing the last building on your right turn right - before the house - to a wooden stile. Keep the hedge on your right to the next stile by a gate. You are now gently descending to Bentley Brook and ahead on the skyline can be seen the clear outline of the site of Hungry Bentley. Descend the field to the bottom righthand corner passing a solitary fenced tree in the middle, to a stile and small bridge over Bentley Brook. Cross and ascend the lefthand side of the field with the hedge on your left. In less than 1/4 mile at the brow of the slope reach a footpath sign on your left. You actually keep straight ahead but before doing so turn right to a stile and onto the site of Hungry Bentley. The house mounds are well defined as is the main street heading east towards Bentley Fields Farm. The owners of the farm have an "Open Farm" arrangement with a Farm Trail around the site and area.

After exploring the site retrace your steps over the stile back to the path sign and turn right to a stile and continue ahead on a track passing the drive entrance to Bentley Fields Farm. Keep ahead to Leapley Lane (named after the Leper Hospital - St. Leonard's Hospital, that existed between Alkmonton and Bentley for looking after female lepers.) Turn right towards Alkmonton. At the junction with the Cubley road is a Millennium oak for Hungry Bentley and Alkmonton, planted September 9th 2000. Continue ahead into the village to the road junction beside the School House, complete with bell. You keep ahead on Leapley Lane, signposted for Boylestone. But first turn left for a few yards to see Alkmonton church dedicated to St. John. The building exterior is unusual for Derbyshire being covered in large pebbles. Inside is the Norman font from the Medieval village of Alkmonton.

Return to Leapley Lane and turn left and in 1/4 mile pass Top House Farm and the course of the Roman Road. Behind the farm is an ancient Fish pond. Continue along the lane down into a small hollow and at the top on the otherside, on your left is the site of Alkmonton village. Again the house mounds and streets can be seen. Continue ahead and a few yards later pass Alkmonton Old Hall on your left.

Just after turn right onto the Boylestone road. In 1/4 mile at the first road on your left opposite a house turn left along it. Approaching the first house - Littleworth Farm - on your right, turn right before it, as footpath signed and stiled. Cross part of the garden to a stile. Cross the field slightly to your right to a gate. On the otherside turn left and keep the hedge on your left to another gate in a few yards and then onto a stile. Here keep the hedge/fence on your right to two stile. Continue ahead with the field boundary (hedge) to your right as it curves round back to you at a stile and footbridge. Keep ahead now with the hedge on your left with Boundary Farm beyond. Continue to a footbridge and onto Ashbourne Road on the council boundary of South Derbyshire - the sign is to your left. Turn right along the road with Potter's Covert on your left and pass Covert Farm. Less than 1/4 mile later pass Bartonpark House on your right. Little over 1/4 mile later on a lefthand curve is an ivy clad footpath sign and stile. Turn right and cross the field to near the far lefthand corner and a stile. Cross the farm track to Gorsty Fields farm to another stile. Pass the farm on your right and beyond keep the hedge on your right to a gate. Cross the next field to a stile and turn right - your goal is the bend in Sapperton lane. Descend the field slightly to your left to a stile and path sign.

Turn right along the lane and soon reach Sapperton Cross (roads). Keep straight ahead - signed Sapperton (Ford). In 150 yards ahead can be seen a house and the field on your left, now ploughed, is the site of Sapperton village. Pass the house and descend lane to Sapperton Manor on your right. Pass the Manor and just after cross the ford and continue on the lane - Marjory Lane - for little over 1/2 mile. To your left is a large pond and at the second drive to Lees Hall Farm turn right to a path sign. Keep to the lefthand path and cross the field aiming to the left of a solitary oak tree, with a stile closeby. To your left, at the top of the field, is the hamlet of Harehill. Continue ahead along the righthand side of the field to a stile and then along the lefthand side of the field to New Road and the white painted - Rose and Crown Inn. Turn left passing a telephone kiosk and the Old Post Office opposite to Chapel Lane on your right. This is also footpath signed - Cubley. Turn right and at Boylestone Methodist Church, turn right to a gate. Cross the field to the far lefthand corner and footbridge over Cubley Brook. Cross and keep the hedge on your left to a gate gap and cheese press stone. Turn left through the gap and keep the hedge on your right to a stile. Just after cross a footbridge as you turn right and keep the hedge on your left as you ascend towards the top of the field. Before the top on your left is a stile. Through this continue ascending past woodland, on your right, to a stile and hedge, with Meadow Hayes Farm on the summit. Turn left and contour round

Cheese Press stone on path below Meadow Hayes Farm.

the field to a gate and descend to a footbridge. Cross and ascend the field with the hedge on your left to a stile and the summit area - you have 360° views from here with the view south to East Staffordshire.

Continue ahead beside the hedge/fence on your left to a gate. Descend the righthand side of the field past a wood on your right to a gate. Continue descending to a stile and gain the track to Brook Farm. Turn right along the track and pass The Old Mill, Cubley on your left before reaching the bend in Cubley road. Keep straight ahead along road to Cubley church dedicated to St. Andrew. Opposite is the site of Cubley Hall. Continue along the road to the crossroads in Great Cubley village, where you began.

Hungry Bentley, Alkmonton and Sapperton - All located on a plateau and all recorded in the Domesday Book (1086 a.d.). Climatic conditions changed with the landscape becoming drier resulting in a severe water shortage, leading to abandonment of the villages.

Domesday Book extractions -

HUNGRY BENTLEY - *"Land for 1 plough. Waste. Value before 1066, 20s (£1) now 11s (55p)."*

ALKMONTON- *"8 villagers and 7 smallholders who have 2 ploughs. Meadow, 12 acres; woodland pasture, 1 league long and 1/2 wide. Value before 1066, 20s (£1); now 11s (55p)."*

34

Sapperton Manor courtyard clocktower.

SAPPERTON - *"Land for 12 oxen. 5 villagers now have 1 plough. Woodland pasture 3 furlongs long and 2 wide. Value now 20s (£1).*

Today, Alkmonton Old Hall is located beside the Medieval village. Sapperton has very little to see but the lane immediately behind the village is very old being delightfully wooded and sunken and a ford. Sapperton Manor keeps the village name alive.

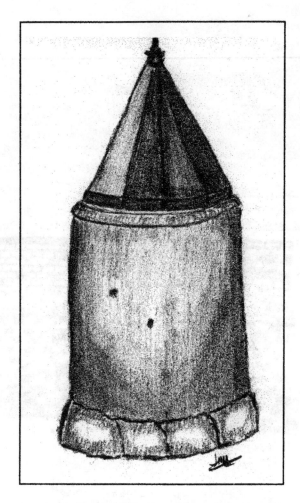

Alkmonton Chuch - Norman font.

ALKMONTON CHURCH, DEDICATED TO ST. JOHN- The church has the Norman font from Alkmonton Medieval village and was found in the area known as Cockshut Croft near the present Alkmonton Old Hall in 1844. The original church was dedicated to St. Alkmund and his sarcophagus can be seen in Derby Museum.

Herringbone masonary,
Cubley Church.

CUBLEY CHURCH, dedicated to St. Andrew - Norman masonry (herringbone) can be seen on the north wall. Inside is a Norman font. On the tower can be seen shields and above the west door are one's to the Montgomery family. The church contains monuments to them and their home, for 400 years, was the moated mansion whose mound and moat outline can be seen opposite, across the road. The moat was recorded waterfilled in 1901. To the left is the outline an ancient fish pond.

Cubley Church - West door and Montgomery shields.

37

BARTON BLOUNT - 6 MILES

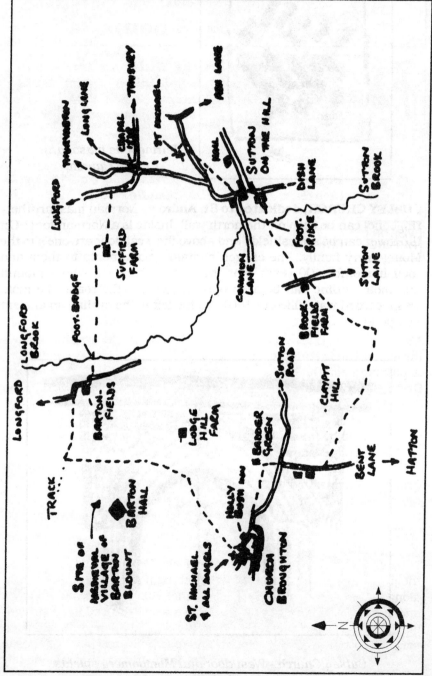

BARTON BLOUNT
- 6 MILES
- allow 2 to 3 hours

Route - Sutton on the Hill - Sutton Brook - Limberstitch Brook - Claypit Hill - The Bent - Badder Green - Church Broughton - Barton Park - Barton Fields Farm - Suffield Farm - Lane Ends - Sutton on the Hill.

Map - 1:25,000 Explorer Series Sheet No.259 - Derbt Uttoxeter, Ashbourne & Cheadle.

Car Park - Roadside parking in Sutton on the Hill.

Inns - Holly Bush Inn, Church Broughton.

ABOUT THE WALK - A wonderful walk in South Derbyshire passing through attractive and historically interesting villages. The main aim is passing near the site of the Mediaeval village of Barton Blount - Grid Ref. SK209346. This is the best known "lost village" which was demolished for the building of today's Barton Hall. Only the original church remains. The path passes near the site. The original house was occupied by the Blount family between the 14th and 16th centuries. The isolated church of Sutton on the Hill, 1/2 mile from the village, is a magnificent vantage point over South Derbyshire. Church Broughton's church dates from Norman times and both churches are well worth a visit, if open. The walk follows mostly little used paths but they are well stiled and signed. On the walk I heard and saw skylarks and lapwings.

WALKING INSTRUCTIONS - Starting from the centre of the village at the junction of Dish Lane near the Cheetham Arms Farm. Keep right along the No Through Road - Brook Lane. This soon becomes a track and leads to a footbridge over Sutton Brook. Cross and keep straight ahead with a hedge to your right to a stile. Then keep the hedge on your left to two more stiles before the road - Sutton Lane - opposite Brookfields Farm. Turn left past the farm then right immediately

39

through a gate - look for the yellow arrows. Cross the field diagonally
left to a footbridge over Limberstich Brook. Continue with a hedge on
your right to a stile and onto another. Here turn right to a stile and
keep along the righthand side of the field to a stile. You are now on the
edge of the Broughton Heath Golf Course. Keep to the right to another
stile and ascend slightly to the top of Claypit Hill - good views from
here. From the "summit" keep the hedge to your left and descend to a
gap and down to a stile. Cross the corner of the field beyond to a stile
and Bent Lane. Turn right and follow the lane to its junction with
Sutton Lane. Go straight across to a stile and walk along the lefthand
side of the field and turn left to a stile. Over this continue ahead on a
track (westwards) from Badder Green farm to the Main Street in Church
Broughton. Where the road forks keep right past the Holly Bush Inn
to Chapel Lane on your right. But before turning here the parish
church, dedicated to St. Michael and All Angels is just ahead opposite
Boggy Lane!

Walk along Chapel Lane past the Methodist Chapel dated 1828 to a
stile and pat sign. Bear right and walk to the far lefthand corner of the
field to a stile.Keep to the righthand side of the field near a hedge and
ascend to a small coppice and stile. Turn left through the coppice to
the road to Barton Hall. Cross via stiles with the hall and church to
your left. Cross the field to the righthand side of another coppice and
stile. Now heading due north keep the fence on your left to a stile.
Keep the hedge on your left at first then it is on your right with the site
of the mediaeval village of Barton Blount on your left; although there
is very little to be seen. The path becomes more defined and becomes
a track and meets another. Here turn right and descend the track to a
road. Follow the road round to your left to Bartonfields Farm. Follow
the road a few more yards round a righthand bend to a stile and path
sign on your left; ahead to your right can be seen the spire of Sutton
on the Hill church, your destination. Keep to the lefthand side of the
field to a footbridge over Longford Brook. Keep straight ahead (eastwards) to a gate and cross the next field to a footbridge and pine trees.
Walk through the trees to a stile and continue to two more with Suffield
Farm on your right. Turn right to the farm and stiles and turn left
along the farm drive to Longford Lane at Lane Ends.

Turn right along the lane and follow it round to your left. Pass Crop-
per Lane on your left, then Back Lane with as chapel dated 1838.
Just past the house on your right turn right to a stile and cross the
field to your right to a stile. Over this ascend directly to the church,
dedicated to St. Michael, using the stiles. Walk through the churchyard to the lane and observe the 360 degree view from here. Cross to
your right to a kissing gate and bear right to the far lefthand side of

the field and a gate. Pass a pond on your right and the castellated Sutton Hall and cricket field to your left to a stile. Walk between the houses to the road and turn left back to the centre at Cheetham Arms Farm where you began.

BURTON BLOUNT -

Named -Bartune in - The Domesday Book (1086) records -

> *"Land for 4 ploughs. 19 villagers and 11 smallholders who have 7 ploughs. A priest and a church; 2 mills, 20s (£1); meadow, 64 acres. Value now £4."*

In the 13th. century the manor was held by Bakepuze of the de Ferrers and the village became known as - Barton Bakepuze. The suffix changed when Sir Walter Blount purchased the manor and others in 1381.

The village lies around the 300 foot contour level on red boulder clay. The land is reasonably dry and is believed to afforded good pasture and crops; although some fields would have made ploughing hard. The village was occupied between the 10th and 15th century. The site has been excavated and a full report of some 100 pages by Guy Beresford in "The Medieval Clay-land Village: Excavations at Goltho and Barton Blount". Published by The Society of Medieval Archaeology Monograph Series No. 6, London 1975. The report details the site in great detail and records 43 crofts in the settlement. Today only the hall and church remain. The Manor House (hall) was occupied by Parliamentary Troops in the Civil War and both the church and manor were badly damaged in 1645/6. Bother were rebuilt in the early 18th century. The hall has since been considerably altered and the church almost abandoned. Originally a moat encircled the hall but this was filled in and landscaped in the early part of the 20th century.

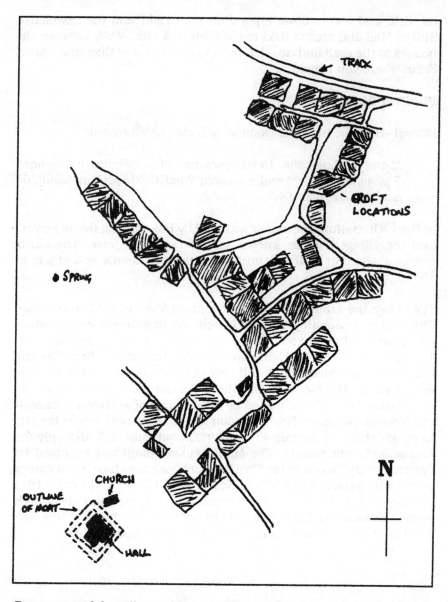

Basic map of the village of Barton Blount, showing crofts and streets.
The walk takes you along the righthand side of the map to the track
at the top.

Remember and observe the Country Code

Enjoy the countryside and respect its life and work.

Guard against all risk of fire.

Fasten all gates.

Keep your dogs under close control.

Keep to public paths across farmland.

Use gates and stiles to cross fences, hedges and walls.

Leave livestock, crops and machinery alone.

Take your litter home - pack it in; pack it out.

Help to keep all water clean.

Protect wildlife, plants and trees.

Take special care on country roads

Make no unnecessary noise.

43

HOLLINGTON, OSLESTON AND LONGFORD - 9 MILES

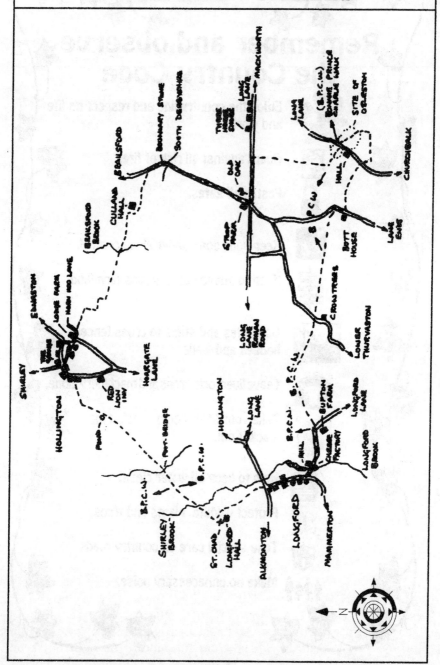

HOLLINGTON, OSLESTON, AND LONGFORD
- 9 MILES
- allow 4 hours.

Route - Hollington - Culland Hall - Stoop Farm - Long Lane - Osleston - Butt House - Bonnie Prince Charlie Walk - Bupton Farm - Longford - Longford Hall - Shirley Brook - Hollington.

Map - 1:25,000 Explorer Series No. 259 - Derby.

Car Park - None. Limited roadside parking in Hollington.

Inns - The Three Horseshoes, Long Lane; just off the route. Red Lion Inn, Hollington; just off the route.

ABOUT THE WALK - The principal aim of the walk is to see Osleston, the largest Medieval village site in Derbyshire. In doing so there is much to see on the walk. You start from the attractive village of Hollington, which has no church, before crossing the fields to Culland Hall. From here you walk along a lane to Long Lane, the line of a Roman Road from Derby to Rocester, before crossing fields to the site of the Medieval village of Osleston. Soon afterwards you join the Bonnie Prince Charlie Walk to Bupton Farm, the sole reminder of Bupton village; a climatic or sheep clearance site. Here you purposely road walk through the present Longford village to pass the delightful Longford Mill with Longford Cheese Factory, the first in England, on your left. Finally across the fields you gain Longford Hall and church on the original Longford village site - village removed to make way for the building of the hall and surrounding parkland. 1 1/2 miles of walking across the fields returns you to Hollington.

WALKING INSTRUCTIONS - Starting from the Shirley road junction. beside The Grange, in Hollington. Turn right along Main Street and right again onto another lane and pass Barn Farm on your right. Just after keep right to Lodge Farm. Here the lane turns right but keep

45

ahead, as footpath signed, along the lane, Horn Hoo. In a few yards this turns left and on your right is a gate. Go through and keep along the righthand side of the field (hedge) to a stile. Turn right and continue on a hedged path to a stile. Turn left and keep a hedge on your left to a gate. Cross the large field bearing slightly right aiming for a gap on the left of a solitary oak tree. Continue ahead across the next field to a stile and bridge over Brailsford Brook. Keep ahead to a gate on the right of a triangular shaped wood, and ascend gently on a track towards Culland Hall. Reach a gate and turn right along a hedged pathway walking around the hall to a gate. Pass the front of the hall with a haa haa on your left, bearing slightly left down to a stile, with a pond well to your right. Continue to two more stiles and path sign by the lane from Cullandmanor Farm to your left. Turn right along the lane and soon pass a boundary stone on your left, by a brook, and step into South Derbyshire. Follow the lane for 1/2 mile to Stoop Farm and junction with Long Lane (line of Roman Road.) On your left is a large old oak tree.

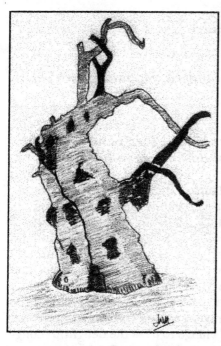

Turn left along Long Lane and in 1/4 mile just before the village sign, Long Lane, turn right over a stile, by a path sign. Keep the hedge on your left to a stile and onto two more before gaining a footbridge. Continue ahead to a field gap and a few yards later bear left to a footbridge - you are now on a section of Bonnie Prince Charlie Walk. Cross the field ascending slightly to your left; in doing so cross the mounds of the site Osleston Medieval village site, to a road. Turn left then right over a stile and leave the "Charlie" walk and bear right across the field, crossing more of the village site. At the other side of the field turn right along the field edge (hedge) and pass a line of trees and ascend to the corner of the field. Turn right, keeping the hedge on your left to the next field corner and a stile. Over this turn right and walk through a farm to the Osleston road, opposite Grass Croft. Turn right then left to a gate and continue along a sunken lane. After the "lane" continue ahead at first by a hedge on your left then ahead to the hedged corner of a field on your right. Bear slightly left across the next field aiming for the solitary Butt House, and a stile and pathsign by the road. Turn right and just before the first corner turn left through a gate and cross to your right to a stile. Bear left and keep the hedge on your left to a bridge. Bear slightly right and ascend the field to the top lefthand corner to a gate and rejoin the Bonnie Prince Charlie Walk. Cross a track to a stile and descend the field to a hedge and ascend gently by it on your right to a stile and lane with Crowtrees Farm on your left.

Go straight across to a stile, still on the "Charlie" signed walk, and cross the large field passing close to a pond on your left before keeping a hedge on your right to a stile and three-way path sign. Bear left then right to a stile, with the large building - The Grange - ahead to your right. descend the field with the hedge on your right to Longford Lane, opposite Bupton Farm; here you leave the "Charlie" walk. Turn right then left along the lane into Longford. In less than 1/4 mile pass Longford Mill with the former wooden Longford Cheese Factory on your left. Cross Longford Brook with the Mill Pond to your right and follow the lane round to your right - Main Street. Pass Longford school on your left to reach the road junction (Hoargate Lane). Go straight across to a gate and pathsign and follow the defined path to a footbridge. Pass a waterfall from the end of Longford Hall lake and pass the hall gates to reach the farm drive. Turn left to the church, dedicated to St. Chad.

On the righthand side of the church is a 3-way path sign, turn right and pass the farm buildings of the hall on a track to a gate. Keep ahead and cross Shirley Brook to a 4-way path sign and cross the Bonnie Prince Charlie Walk. You are now following the final path back to Hollington, which is little used! First cross the field to the righthand side of wood to a stile and footbridge. Bear slightly left crossing the field to a gap in the hedge less than 1/4 mile away. Continue aiming for the far "top" lefthand corner of the field, where there is a stile. To your right is a solitary barn. Cross the next field and pass on the righthand side of a pond to reach a gate. Cross the next field to a gate just beyond the hedged righthand corner of the field and turn right for Hollington. Keep the hedge on your right to a gate and on towards the village. Go through a stile and walk along a garden path to reach the Main Street - the Red Lion Inn is well to your right. Turn left to pass the telephone kiosk before the Shirley road junction, where you began.

OSLESTON - At the time of the Domesday Book, Osleston -

> *"Ernwy and Leofwin had 12 b. of land taxable.*
> *Land for 3 ploughs. Now in lordship 2 ploughs.*
> *12 villagers and 4 smallholders who have 3 ploughs.*
> *Woodland pasture 1/2 league long and 4 furlongs wide.*
> *Value before 1066, 60s (£3); now 40s (£2). John holds it."*

The church of Sutton on the Hill, nearby, contains the registers for Osleston. One fascinating entry in 1593 records -

"1593 - Alice Cather a poore woman of Osliston choked, or as some supposed beinge drunke fell downe flatt upon her face and so stopped her breath and was buried the 2 of September. A caveat for all drinkers, gluttons and beastley belliegods, to beware of god's severe judgement agaynst them" - please note original spelling.

BONNIE PRINCE CHARLIE WALK - Traces Bonnie Prince Charlie's march from Ashbourne to Derby, in 1745. The Derby Museum has a room dedicated to the Prince.

LONGFORD CHEESE FACTORY - The first cheese factory in England, opened in 1870. The largely wooden building has a plaque recording this event.

LONGFORD HALL - Originally owned by the Longford family and in the 17th. century, the Coke family.

LONGFORD CHURCH, dedicated to St. Chad - Mostly 15th century with monuments to the Longford and Coke families.

Longford Mill.

Longford Cross - the upper portion above sketch, was added in 1897.

DERVENTIO AND DARLEY ABBEY
- 4 MILES

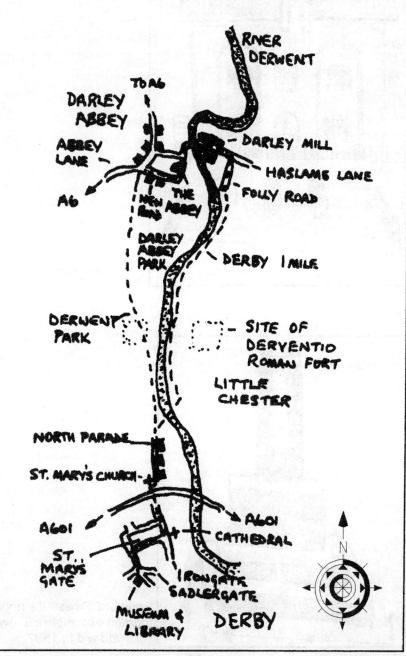

RIVER DERWENT

TO A6

DARLEY ABBEY

ABBEY LANE

A6

NEW ZEALAND

THE ABBEY

DARLEY ABBEY PARK

DARLEY MILL

HASLAMS LANE

FOLLY ROAD

DERBY 1 MILE

DERWENT PARK

SITE OF DERVENTIO ROMAN FORT

LITTLE CHESTER

NORTH PARADE

ST. MARY'S CHURCH

A601

ST. MARY'S GATE

A601

CATHEDRAL

IRONGATE
SADLERGATE

MUSEUM & LIBRARY

DERBY

N

DERBY - DERVENTIO (Roman Fort) and DARLEY ABBEY
- 4 miles
- allow 2 to 3 hours.

Route - Darley Abbey - Darley Abbey Park - Derwent Park - Strutt's Park Roman Fort Site - St. Mary's Church - Derby Museum - St. Mary's Church - Little Chester - Site of Derventio Roman Fort - Darley Mill - Site of Darley Abbey - Darley Abbey.

Map - 1:25,000 Explorer Series No. 259 - Derby.

Car Park - Roadside parking in Darley Abbey - Abbey Lane.

Inns & Teas -
The Abbey Inn, Darley Dale.
Teas in Darley Park. Numerous in Derby.

ABOUT THE WALK - A short *"town walk"* to the north of central Derby to Darley Abbey, exploring the east and western sides of the River Derwent, the site of the Roman Fort - Derventio. I have started the walk from the junction of New Road and Abbey Lane in Darley Abbey but you can start from central Derby. First you walk down the western side of the River Derwent to Derwent Park and the site of Strutt's park Roman Fort site. You continue heading towards Derby and passing your route across the river to Little Chester. Before doing this you head into central Derby to Derby Museum which has displays and finds from the Roman period helping you appreciate what existed here before today's occupation. You retrace your steps and cross the river and walk past the site Derventio Roman Fort. You continue on the eastern side of the river and to regain Darley Abbey you walk through the historical Darley Mill. In Darley Abbey you see the last remaining building of Darley Abbey before ascending New Road back to the start. Derventio was the largest Roman Fort in Derbyshire and Darley Abbey the biggest monastic site.

WALKING INSTRUCTIONS - Starting from the junction of New Road and Abbey Lane in Darley Abbey, turn left and ascend a tarmaced walled path. On your left is the entrance to Darley Park with a tea-room. Follow this path soon with views of the River Derwent and Darley Park on your left. In about 1/2 mile nearing a "hollow" in the path line, to your right up some steps is an Information Plaque to Strutts Park and site of the Roman Fort here. The river was crossed here by a Roman Bridge into the Derventio Roman Fort opposite. Continue on the walled tarmaced path and in 1/4 mile pass the Derwent Rowing Club down on your left, beside the river. Continue ahead ascending slightly to North Parade road and on your left is the path/cycleway to Little Chester. But before crossing keep ahead along North Parade and its elegant houses on your left. Keep straight ahead into Darley Lane and at the end turn left to St. Mary's Roman Catholic church. The church tower and one across road, Derby Cathedral, acts as guides. A visit to St. Mary's - door on your right - is worthwhile to see the red window to the six Derby Martyrs. Turn left and cross the bridge over the A601 and descend to the underpass at the end. Through it, turn right to continue heading towards Derby Cathedral. Pass the site of John Smith's Clockworks on your right. Opposite the cathedral turn right down St. Mary's Gate. At the bottom left along Bold Lane to Derby Museum.

After your visit retrace your steps along Bold Lane, St. Mary's Gate to the cathedral. Turn left and head towards St. Mary's church descending on the right to the underpass, and cross the footbridge to the church. Turn right then left along Darley Lane and continue along North Parade. At the end turn right following the cycleway path to Little Chester across an old railway bridge. At the end of the bridge turn left and follow the path beside river and in 1/4 mile on your right is the site of Derventio, Roman Fort. Continue beside the river and in less than 1/2 mile cross a bridge into Folly Lane. Turn right along it and at the top, turn left along Haslams Lane and walk through Darley Mill into Darley Abbey. Turn left and soon reach the last standing piece of Darley Abbey, aptly named "The Abbey", with inn sign of monks. A few more strides and turn right and ascend New Road to its junction with Abbey Lane, where you began.

DERVENTIO - ROMAN FORT - There are two Roman forts, situated on opposite sides of the River Derwent.

Strutts Park (SK319471) - Now located in Derwent Park on the west bank of the river. The timber fort was built in about 50 AD and was a frontier post on the borders of the Roman Province and the native kingdom of the Brigantes. The fort controlled the area where two Roman Roads crossed the river - one eastwards from Sawley to Rocester and the other northwards - Ryknield Street - linking Wall (Staffordshire) with Chesterfield and Templeborough (Rotherham). The foundations of a bridge is thought to lie in the river bed. In about 80 AD the Roman Governor, Julius Agricola, moved northwards to occupy Brigantian country and a new supply base was needed and built opposite at Little Chester.

Little Chester (SK353375) - Built on the east bank of the river between there and the railway. A 4th century Roman walled enclosure was found and measured last century - approximately 600 feet x 500 feet. The site was occupied to the 5th century. A Roman Bath was found south of the walled enclosure. Passing its eastern side was Ryknield Street and Derventio lay at the halfway point between the Roman forts at Wall and Templeborough.

Finds from the forts can be seen in Derby Museum.

DARLEY MILL - Dates from 1783 when the Evans family built a cotton mill here. Prior to this there was a copper and iron mill. In the early 19th century a branch canal linked the mill complex to the Derby Canal.

DARLEY ABBEY - Augustinian Canons - Robert de Ferrers, Earl of Derby, in 1137 AD., gave land to the church to build an abbey here. Over the centuries the Abbey became very prosperous with considerable land and buildings throughout Derbyshire. Eventually it was the richest and most powerful in Derbyshire and central England. Like all monasteries in the 16th century with the Dissolution of Monasteries it came to an abrupt end; more fully than others in Derbyshire. The trouble began in 1534 when Henry V111 asked all monks to -

i. Acknowledge him as the Head of the English Church.

ii. Confirm the legality of his marriage to Anne Boleyn.

Failure would result in the closure of the Abbey and all its property confiscated.

At first the Abbey survived but in 1536 the Act of Suppression was introduced. whereby all monasteries with an income of £200 per annum or less were to be dissolved and their property became the King's. Darley Abbey's income was more than £200 per annum and at first survived but two years later on October 22nd. 1538 the Abbey closed with the surrender of the Abbot and his thirteen monks. The Abbey's income that year was £258. 14s 5d (£258.72p). The contents and building stone were sold. Today only "The Abbey Inn" remains. The building is thought to have been used as a guest house.

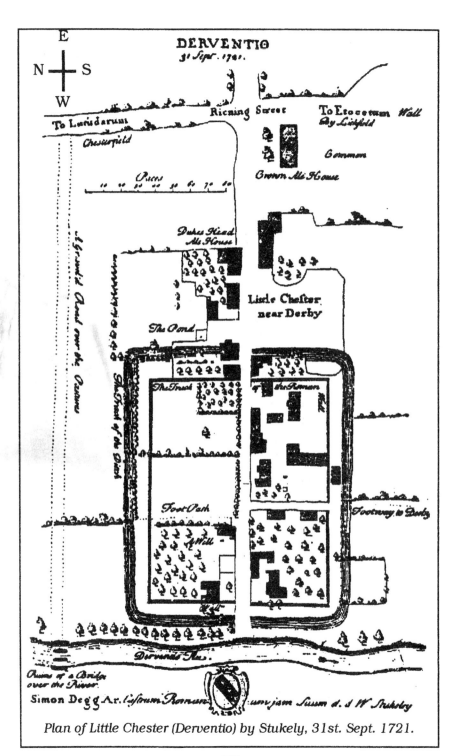

Plan of Little Chester (Derventio) by Stukely, 31st. Sept. 1721.

REPTON, INGLEBY AND FOREMARK
- 9 MILES

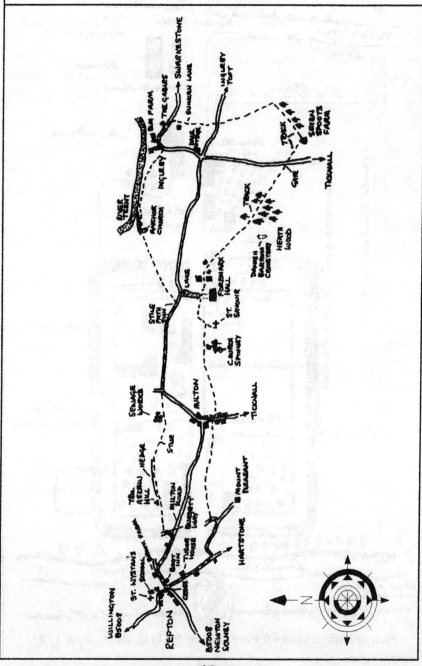

REPTON, INGLEBY AND FOREMARK
- 9 MILES
- allow 4 to 5 hours.

 Route - Repton - Askew Hill, 78m. - Windmill Hill - Anchor Church - River Trent - Ingleby - Seven Spouts Farm - Heath Wood - Foremark Hall & Church - Church Spinney - Milton - Repton.

 Map - 1:25,000 Explorer Series No. 245 - The National Forest.

 Car Park - Beside church.

 Inns - Boot Inn and Red Lion Inn; Repton. One in Milton off the route.

 Teas - Brook Farm Tea Room, Brook Lane, Repton.

ABOUT THE WALK - There is much to see on this walk, hence the time to be allowed. Repton is well worth exploring with the church and Saxon Crypt and opposite the Priory remains, now part of Repton School. Repton was the capital of Mercia. First you cross fields with 360° views and pass views to Foremark Hall and church, before descending to Anchor Church - a hermit's cave - and the River Trent. You reach the hamlet of Ingleby, whose location is a result of sheep clearances. Following tracks through woodland you head back westwards to Repton to Foremark Hall and church before reaching Milton. You cross a handful of fields and descend to the southern side of Repton and walk into the centre passing places of interest, including The Tudor House and Market Cross. I suggest you explore Repton church, dedicated to St. Wystan, at the end.The walk combines monastic, sheep clearance and wealthy landowners, " lost villages".

WALKING INSTRUCTIONS - Starting from the church and entrance gateway (Priory Gateway) to Repton School, continue along the main road towards the Market Cross, but soon turn left down Brook End, keeping the tall and solid Priory wall on your left. In a few strides pass Boot Inn on your right and interestingly named Boot Hill - for a moment you make think you are in the wild west! Continue ahead and pass an arch in the wall on your left - this was moved - 9 yards north - to its present position in March 1905. Originally water for the Priory Mill flowed under it. Pass Brook Farm (tearoom) on your left and just after follow the road round, sharply, to your right; now on Milton Road. Continue on the road for nearly 1/4 mile to the second road on your left, the aptly named, Burdett Way. Turn left and before house no. 12, turn right as footpath signed and pass between the houses to a stile. Continue ahead on the defined path to a stile and then along a hedged path to a stile with a clump of trees and triangulation pillar on your left - the summit of Askew Hill, 78 metres. The views are extensive here over southern Derbyshire. Continue with the hedge on your left and as you descend you can see a Sewage plant - your path leads to the righthand side of it! First descend to a stile and footbridge and bear slightly right to a stile and onto the righthand side of the plant. Over the stile bear left along a fenced path to a gate. Keep to the righthand side on the field to a stile and path sign at a bend in the Milton-Ingleby road.

Turn left along the road and follow it for 1/2 mile. In 1/4 mile you have views to your right to Foremark church, which you will pass later. Pass the HGV entrance to Foremark Hall and a few yards later with Foremark Hall's school's playing fields on your right (over the hedge), turn left over a stile by a path sign. The hall can be seen and again you pass this later. Cross the field to your right keeping to the high ground before descending to a stile. Turn right and follow the path which soon passes beneath the prominent cliffs, which soon have stone buttresses. In 1/4 mile with an arm of the River Trent (Black Pool) on your left reach the carved Anchor Church - explore its rooms and windows. Continue on the path and bear right then left to walk above the cliffs before descending to the River Trent. Continue by the river to a stile and turn right then left keeping a fence on your right as you ascend the cliffs to solitary pines and oaks. The delightful hamlet of Ingleby comes into view and guided by stiles keep to the right of it. Above the houses reach a stile and bear right down the field to a gate, path sign, and road through a small dale.

Turn left and walk through the village past Elm Farm and opposite The Gables, turn right and ascend a house drive - bridlepath signed. Pass the house on your right and keep ahead on a sunken lane to a gate. Keep to the lefthand side of the field with the hedge on your left to a gate and lane. Go straight across to another gate and continue with the hedge on your right to a bridlepath sign. Bear slightly left and cross the middle of the field on a path before descending to your right to a holly tree, bridlepath sign and track. Turn right along the track through woodland, passing a fishing pond on your left, to Seven Spout Farm. Turn right and continue on a track, soon with extensive views to your right (northwards), to a lane. Go straight across to a gate and continue ahead on a track to a stile on the edge of Heath Wood. Keep ahead now descending through the wood on the track to a gate and stile at its western end. Continue on the track with trees on your right and in more than 1/4 mile pass the greenhouse area on your left and private houses on your right as you enter Foremark Hall complex. Basically keep straight ahead on the school drive which soon curves right to the front of the hall with lake on your right. Keep on the drive - still a right of way - and walk through woodland to a track junction - the HGV entrance you passed earlier. Turn left and ascend the track to Foremark Church. Just before it notice on your right a path leading to the righthand side of Church Spinney - this is your route after visiting the church.

Explore the church and return to the path junction and turn left across the field to the righthand side of Church Spinney. Keep ahead across the next field to a stile. Descend the next field slightly to your left to a stile and onto more before gaining the road in Milton village. Turn right and in a few yards pass Kirkby Holt and turn left, as footpath signed, and walk through Common Farm to a hedged path. Keep ahead soon with the hedge on your right to a stile. The path is defined as you cross the next field to a stile and onto another before walking between the houses to enter Repton. Turn left along Springfield Road to its junction with Mount Pleasant Road. Turn right along this road which later becomes Pinfold Road. Follow it round to your left to its junction with High Street with a shop opposite established in 1842. Turn right along the High Street towards central Repton. Pass Tudor Lodge on your right and at the Market Cross turn right towards the church and start of the walk.

ANCHOR CHURCH - Believed to have been occupied by St. Hardulph of Breedon in the 7th century - the prominent church on Breedon Hill is dedicated to him. The Repton Parish Register has an entry in 1658- *"Ye foole at Anchor Church bur. April 19"* This probably helps to fuel the notion that a hermit lived here. Close to the main cave is a smaller one known as the "Anchorite's Larder." The cave was popular with Sir Francis Burdett who held parties here on summer evenings. He had the caves enlarged and a door fitted; hence the stone recess on the main entrance.

INGLEBY - The Domesday Book records, (their are unusually four entries) -

"In Ingleby 3 b. of land taxable. Land for 4 oxen. Jurisdiction in Repton.
3 Freemen have 1 plough.
Meadow, 4 acres; marshland, 1 acre; woodland pasture in Ticknall 1 league long and 1/2 league wide."

" 1 villager and 2 smallholders with 1/2 plough."

" 3 villagers and 2 smallholders have 1 plough.
Meadow, 7 acres; 1 mill site.
Value 10s (50p)"

FOREMARK HALL - Built by Sir Robert Burdett in 1755. The Palladian style building was designed by David Hiorns of Warwick.

FOREMARK VILLAGE - Recorded in the Domesday Book -

"In Foremark Ulfkell had 2 c. of land taxable. Land for 2 ploughs. Now in Lordship 1 plough.
5 villagers and 3 smallholders have 1 plough.
1 mill, 2s (10p); meadow, 24 acres; woodland pasture 1/2 league long and as wide.
Value before 1066, 40s (£2); now 15s (75p)."

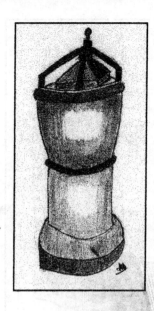

ST. SAVIOUR'S CHURCH, FOREMARK - The church was consecrated in 1662 and was built by Sir Francis Burdett. The church served the old villages of Foremark and Ingleby. The stone for the churchyard walls came from the ruined Ingleby chapel. The 13th century pillared font is believed to have come from Ingleby chapel. Many believe the church was the first to be built following the restoration of the Monarchy. The interior has box pews, a three decker pulpit and Burdett hatchments with their coat of arms and motto - "Cleave Fast." The gates, at the rear of the church, leading down to the hall are by Robert Bakewell of Derby.

TUDOR HOUSE, REPTON - Timbered framed house with two storied porch and believed to date from the end of the 16th century. The timbers rest on the stone plinths from Repton Priory.

REPTON CROSS - Medieval Market Cross; Wednesday was Market Day. The old Midland custom of "Wife Selling" was carried out here in 1848, when a man from Burton Upon Trent brought his wife with a halter around her waist and sold her for one shilling (5p)!

CHURCH, DEDICATED TO ST. WYSTAN'S - One of the most interesting church's in Derbyshire with its Saxon Crypt. There are many monuments through the ages and different architectural styles; mostly 13th and 14th centuries. The crypt is reached via steps on the lefthand side just before the chancel.

SAXON CRYPT - The finest Saxon Crypt in England. Repton was the capital of Mercia in the 7th century and was where Saxon Kings and Queen's were buried. King Ethelbald of Mercia was interred here in 757 AD. King Wiglaf in 840 and when his grandson, the Saxon prince, Wystan was killed he too was buried here. His shrine became known for its miracles. In 875 AD the Danes plundered the area destroying the monastery and part of the crypt. This was later rebuilt but over centuries it became "lost". It was not until 1779 when a grave digger was digging a hole in the church chancel that he fell through the floor into the crypt!

REPTON PRIORY - The archway dates from the 13th century. The Old Priory of the Augustinian canons dates from 1172 AD. The Priory was destroyed at the Dissolution. In 1557 this became Repton School and is still in use today. Remains can still be seen of the Priory church and guest house. The public are allowed in to view these.

63

A selection of other Lost Village locations -

BALLIDON - SK203645 - Lies just to the south of the present Ballidon of three farms. A monastic clearance with just the chapel in the field remaining. Around it spreading westwards onto the otherside of the road can be seen mounds - house platforms - and hollows - streets. A right of way - east to west - from Parwich, crosses the site; as does a north to south route from Bradbourne to Ballidon.

ILAM - SK134507 - Although in Staffordshire it is in the Peak District National park, close to Dovedale and the Manifold Valley. The church dating back to Saxon times is the only building left. The village being "removed" by the wealthy landowner in the late 18th century to create parkland.

CHEE TOR - SK127734 - Marked on the White Peak map - "Settlement" - this is a late prehistoric habitation, with hut circles and field systems. The mounds cane be seen on the ground, but like all lost village sites they are best seen from the air! A right of way from Wormhill to Blackwell passes the eastern side of the site.

STEETLEY - SK543788 - Lying in the north-eastern corner of Derbyshire, just off the A619, three miles east of Worksop, is the solitary but magnificent Steetley Chapel. The mediaeval village lies in the next field to the west. This is an example of plague depopulation. The Black Death in 1349/50 raged through England, Europe and Asia with some 50 million people dying from it. In Derbyshire 77 priests died and 22 resigned. Here in Steetley the priest, Lawrence Le Leche, who came here in 1348, stayed to care for the sick and dying; becoming known as "Le Leche". A nearby stream gave them pure water. He stayed for seven years before dying himself. His tomb was infront of the porch so that people coming to the church never forgot to bless him! The village was deserted and the survivors moved to Whitwell to live.. Remarkably more than 300 years later the Rev William Mompesson was to carry out a similar act in Eyam.

The Norman church, dedicated to All Saints, is believed to have been built in about 1175 by Gley le Breton and is Derbyshire finest Norman building. Sadly it left abandoned for 300 years with the roof fallen in. The chapel - only 56 feet long - was restored in the late 19th century and has an exceptional Norman Apse.

Inside the chapel is the stone slab tomb of Lawrence le Leche. The carving shows an altar with three legs above which is a chalice, paten and hand extended in blessing.

Museums -

SHEFFIELD CITY MUSEUM,
Weston Park,
Sheffield,
South Yorkshire
S10 2TP

Tel. 0114 - 278 2600

BUXTON MUSEUM & ART GALLERY,
Terrace Road,
Buxton,
Derbyshire.
SK17 6DA

Tel. 01298 - 24658
Fax. 01298 - 79394

DERBY MUSEUM & ART GALLERY,
The Strand,
Derby
DE1 1BS

Tel. 01332 - 716659

CHESTERFIELD MUSEUM,
St. Mary's Gate,
Chesterfield
Derbyshire

Tel. 01246 - 345727

ABOUT THE WALKS

Whilst every care is taken detailing and describing the walk in this book, it should be borne in mind that the countryside changes by the seasons and the work of man. I have described the walk to the best of my ability, detailing what I have found on the walk in the way of stiles and signs. Obviously with the passage of time stiles become broken or replaced by a ladder stile or even a small gate. Signs too have a habit of being broken or pushed over. All the route follow rights of way and only on rare occasions will you have to overcome obstacles in its path, such as a barbed wire fence or electric fence. On rare occasions rights of way are rerouted and these ammendments are included in the next edition.

The seasons bring occasional problems whilst out walking which should also be borne in mind. In the height of summer paths become overgrown and you will have to fight your way through in a few places. In low lying areas the fields are often full of crops, and although the pathline goes straight across it may be more practical to walk round the field edge to get to the next stile or gate. In summer the ground is generally dry but in autumn and winter, especially because of our climate, the surface can be decidedly wet and slippery; sometimes even gluttonous mud! Flooding is sometimes a problem and alternatives are described.

These comments are part of countryside walking which help to make your walk more interesting or briefly frustrating. Standing in a farmyard up to your ankles in mud might not be funny at the time but upon reflection was one of the highlights of the walk!

The mileage for each section is based on three calculations -

1. pedometer reading.
2. the route map measured on the map.
3. the time I took for the walk.

I believe the figure stated for each section to be very accurate but we all walk differently and not always in a straight line! The time allowed for each section is on the generous side and does not include pub stops etc. The figure is based on the fact that on average a person walks 2 1/2 miles an hours but less in hilly terrain.

67

WALK RECORD CHART

Date walked -

Derwent and Ashopton - 11 miles ....

Calton, Edensor and Chatsworth - 4 miles ....

Conksbury - 3 miles ....

Middleton and Gratton - 10 miles ....

Roystone Grange - 3 miles ....

Great Cubley and three Medieval Lost Villages - 11 miles ....

Barton Blount - 8 miles ....

Hollington, Osleston and Longford - 9 miles ....

Derby - Derventio and Darley Abbey - 4 miles ....

Repton, Ingleby and Foremark - 9 miles ....

Some other "lost village" locations ....

JOHN MERRILL WALK BADGE

THE JOHN MERRILL WALK BADGE

Complete six walks in this book and get the above special embroidered badge and signed certificate. Badges are black cloth with lettering and man embroidered in four colours.

BADGE ORDER FORM

Date walks completed...

NAME ....

ADDRESS ....

....

Price: £3.50 each including postage, VAT and signed completion certificate. Amount enclosed (Payable to *Walk & Write Ltd*) ..
From: **Walk & Write Ltd.,**
Unit 1, Molyneux Business Park, Whitworth Road, Darley Dale,
Matlock, Derbyshire. DE45 1JE
Tel /Fax (01629) - 735911
********** *YOU MAY PHOTOCOPY THIS FORM* ***********
"HAPPY WALKING!" T SHIRT
- Yellow (Sunflower) with black lettering and walking man logo.
Send £7.95 to *Walk & Write Ltd.*, stating size required.
John Merrill's "Happy Walking!" Cap - £3.50
Happy Walking Button Badge - 50p inc p & p.

John Merrill's
"My Derbyshire" Historical Series

A TO Z GUIDE TO THE PEAK DISTRICT by John N. Merrill .... 0 907496 89 X....£3.50

WINSTER - A SOUVENIR GUIDE. by John N. Merrill.............. 0907496 81 4.................£2.50.

DERBYSHIRE INNS - AN A TO Z GUIDE. by John N. Merrill........ 0907496 71 7.............£4.50.

HALLS & CASTLES OF THE PEAK DISTRICT. by John N. Merrill....0907496 72 5.....£3.95.

ARKWRIGHT OF CROMFORD by John N. Merrill.............. 0 907496 35 0...............£4.50.

DERBYSHIRE FACTS AND RECORDS by John N. Merrill .... 1 874754 12 8...........£3.00

PEAK DISTRICT PLACE NAMES by Martin Spray ...... 0 907496 82 2.....................£3.25

THE STORY OF THE EYAM PLAGUE by C.Daniel ......ISBN 0 9523444 0 8..£6.95

THE EYAM DISCOVERY TRAIL & 1858 RAMBLE by Clarence Daniel ....£3.50.

PEAK DISTRICT SKETCH BOOK - ....ISBN 1 874754 02 0..£5.00

DERBYSHIRE LOST VILLAGE WALKS £5.95

GHOSTS & LEGENDS -

DERBYSHIRE FOLKLORE. by John N. Merrill...........0 907496 31 8..............................£5.95.

DERBYSHIRE PUNISHMENT by John N. Merrill....................0 907496 33 4.............£3.00.

CUSTOMS OF THE PEAK DISTRICT & DERBYS by J. N. Merrill .... 0 907496 34 2.....£3.50

LEGENDS OF DERBYSHIRE. by John N. Merrill...............1 874754 00 4..........................£3.95

NEW TITLES IN PREPARATION -

LOST INDUSTRIES OF DERBYSHIRE by John N. Merrill £6.95

DERBYSHIRE HISTORY THROUGH THE AGES -

Vol 3 - DERBYSHIRE IN NORMAN TIMES by John N. Merrill £4.50

Vol 1 - DERBYSHIRE IN PREHISTORIC TIMES by John N. Merrill £4.50

CHURCHES OF DERBYSHIRE by John N. Merrill £4.95

DERBYSHIRE IN MONASTIC TIMES by John N. Merrill £4.50

OTHER JOHN MERRILL WALK BOOKS

NORTH YORKSHIRE MOORS CHALLENGE WALK
LAKELAND CHALLENGE WALK
THE RUTLAND WATER CHALLENGE WALK
MALVERN HILLS CHALLENGE WALK
THE SALTER'S WAY
THE SNOWDON CHALLENGE
CHARNWOOD FOREST CHALLENGE WALK
THREE COUNTIES CHALLENGE WALK (Peak District).
CAL-DER-WENT WALK by Geoffrey Carr,
THE QUANTOCK WAY
BELVOIR WITCHES CHALLENGE WALK
THE CARNEDDAU CHALLENGE WALK
THE SWEET PEA CHALLENGE WALK

INSTRUCTION & RECORD -
HIKE TO BE FIT.....STROLLING WITH JOHN
THE JOHN MERRILL WALK RECORD BOOK
HIKE THE WORLD

MULTIPLE DAY WALKS -
THE RIVERS'S WAY
PEAK DISTRICT: HIGH LEVEL ROUTE
PEAK DISTRICT MARATHONS
THE LIMEY WAY
THE PEAKLAND WAY
COMPO'S WAY by Alan Hiley

COAST WALKS & NATIONAL TRAILS -
ISLE OF WIGHT COAST PATH
PEMBROKESHIRE COAST PATH
THE CLEVELAND WAY
WALKING ANGELSEY'S COASTLINE.

MY DERBYSHIRE HISTORICAL GUIDES -
A to Z GUIDE OF THE PEAK DISTRICT
DERBYSHIRE INNS - an A to Z guide
HALLS AND CASTLES OF THE PEAK DISTRICT & DERBYSHIRE
TOURING THE PEAK DISTRICT & DERBYSHIRE BY CAR
DERBYSHIRE FOLKLORE
PUNISHMENT IN DERBYSHIRE
CUSTOMS OF THE PEAK DISTRICT & DERBYSHIRE
WINSTER - a souvenir guide
ARKWRIGHT OF CROMFORD
LEGENDS OF DERBYSHIRE
DERBYSHIRE FACTS & RECORDS
TALES FROM THE MINES by Geoffrey Carr
PEAK DISTRICT PLACE NAMES by Martin Spray

JOHN MERRILL'S MAJOR WALKS -
TURN RIGHT AT LAND'S END
WITH MUSTARD ON MY BACK
TURN RIGHT AT DEATH VALLEY
EMERALD COAST WALK
JOHN MERRILL'S 1999 WALKER'S DIARY
A WALK IN OHIO - 1,310 miles around the Buckeye Trail

SKETCH BOOKS -
SKETCHES OF THE PEAK DISTRICT

COLOUR BOOK:-
THE PEAK DISTRICT.......something to remember her by.

OVERSEAS GUIDES -
HIKING IN NEW MEXICO - Vol I - The Sandia and Manzano Mountains.
Vol 2 - Hiking "Billy the Kid" Country. Vol 4 - N.W. area - " Hiking Indian Country."
"WALKING IN DRACULA COUNTRY" - Romania.

VISITOR GUIDES - MATLOCK . BAKEWELL. ASHBOURNE.